Don't Be a B*tch, BE AN ALPHA

HOW TO UNLOCK YOUR MAGIC, PLAY BIG, AND CHANGE THE WORLD

Seo Kelleher

Alpha Sisters Publishing

Special Edition ISBN: 978-1-7334756-0-0
Trade Paperback ISBN: 978-1-7334756-1-7
eBook ISBN: 978-1-7334756-2-4

Published by Alpha Sisters Publishing
2540 Professional Road, Suite 6
Richmond, VA 23235

First Edition

Illustrator: Sarah Culclasure
Editor: E. Ce Miller and Meldon Jones
Cover and Book Design: Sarah Culclasure

Publisher's Cataloging-In-Publication Data
(Prepared by The Donohue Group, Inc.)

Names: Kelleher, Seo, author. | Culclasure, Sarah, illustrator.
Title: Don't be a b*tch, be an alpha : how to unlock your magic, play big, and change the world / Seo Kelleher ; [illustrator: Sarah Culclasure].
Other Titles: Don't be a bitch, be an alpha | Do not be a b*tch, be an alpha | Do not be a bitch, be an alpha
Description: First edition. | Richmond, VA : Alpha Sisters Publishing, [2019]
Identifiers: ISBN 9781733475617 (trade paperback) | ISBN 9781733475600 (special edition, full color) | ISBN 9781733475624 (ebook)
Subjects: LCSH: Self-actualization (Psychology) in women. | Women--Conduct of life. | Women--Psychology. | Change (Psychology)
Classification: LCC BF637.S4 K45 2019 (print) | LCC BF637.S4 (ebook) | DDC 158.1--dc23

Printed in the United States of America for Worldwide Distribution

Introduction

....

If you're holding this book in your hands, I'm guessing you're searching for something—even if you're not totally sure what that is yet. Maybe you're looking for strength, confidence, or abundance. Maybe it's emotional or financial security; clarity in the path you've chosen in work or life; or advice on how to balance your energy. Perhaps you're searching for tips on awakening and healing your spirit. Maybe you're just looking for someone who understands you.

You might be at a crossroads in your professional life or in a personal relationship. Maybe you're wondering why no matter how hard you work, you never seem to earn the money or recognition you feel you deserve. Maybe you're constantly finding yourself misunderstood by others and want to learn how to communicate your needs—and who, exactly, you are—in more effective ways. Or you're looking for your tribe and a community of Alpha Women sounds like it might be just the place for you.

Am I on the right track here?

Once upon a time I was looking for all those things too. Now, at 40-something years old, I've found my place as an intuitive coach who helps high-performing women (my "Alpha Sisters") realize their purpose and go after it wholeheartedly. But it wasn't always like this.

I spent most of my early adult life—up until my mid-thirties—living and working in the corporate world, following the rules laid out by mainstream society. Before that, I was your typical over-achieving, straight-A student: a rule follower who did everything (and I mean *everything*) by the book. In my academic life and later, my professional life, it was all about working hard, out-performing my peers, competing for the next promotion, and playing the games required to become a powerful person in my field (but, of course, if you're a woman, not *too* powerful). I was experiencing what others might call "success": making a lot of money, garnering recognition from company leaders, earning leadership roles on important projects.

And yet, I was extremely unhappy.

All around me, I noticed other women who weren't happy either. They were struggling to find their own healthy work/life balance; often working longer and harder than their male peers for less money, few benefits, and even fewer leadership positions. All too often, they were motivated by fear: fear of failure, fear of criticism, fear of exclusion, even fear of success. After a decade of living this kind of life and subscribing to its prescribed belief system, I realized that I wanted out. I wanted to be motivated by something other than fear—even though I didn't know what that was yet. But first, I needed to leave the corporate world in order to explore what it was I really wanted.

That's how I entered the world of entrepreneurship—starting my own fitness company and then becoming a life and business coach. By working with a coach of my own, I began to sort through all of my limiting beliefs, past traumas, and issues with forgiveness. I even tried meditation! Suddenly, things started happening. I was able to hear the call of my own higher self. I found clarity. I discovered the courage to act on that clarity, and that's when everything started to become more magical.

My life and business continued to evolve and expand. I started trusting my intuition and my emerging psychic abilities more, and began incorporating them into my personal and professional life. I started attracting more and more like-minded people: other Alpha Sisters, who were interested in my journey and who I was as a person, each providing their own unique support, camaraderie, and inspiration.

I realized my true passion was connecting with these women and empowering them.

See, the entire time I was building my career and evolving in my professional life, I was repeatedly described as an "alpha"—and at the same time, I was told that I shouldn't be one. According to "them" (the critics, the naysayers) Alpha Women are bossy, opinionated, difficult to work with, untrustworthy around other women, terrible team players, and best avoided altogether. I was advised to tone down who I was in order to "get along" with others or to "get ahead" in my career. Except all of those labels and the idea of toning myself down—none of that rang true to me. And that made me wonder… what if all the narratives about what it means to be an "alpha female" were bullshit? What if, in fact, the opposite were true instead? What would happen if women were actually *encouraged* to embrace their Alpha qualities and actually felt safe to thrive as the powerful, magical boss women that we are? And hey, what if there were a community of other Alpha Women, designed to support collaborative growth, authenticity, and self-expression? Wouldn't that actually be good for the world?

Once I started working for myself—spending years away from the rules and narratives set forth by other people—I realized that everything I'd ever been taught about what it means to be an "alpha female" was bullshit. I was (and AM!) an Alpha—a woman who is strong, capable, passionate, and great leader. All those other labels are ones I don't identify with—and neither do any of my Alpha Sisters. In fact, all those labels are basically describing a bitch—something Alpha Women definitely aren't! Alpha women thrive in the presence of other women. We crave connection and love empowering one another to succeed. And that's why my organization—the Alpha Female Sisterhood—was created. I didn't have a space where I felt safe and supported as my authentic self, so I created one. And, as it turned out, lots of other women were looking for that kind of space too.

This is still a work in progress. As someone who used to need rules to follow, exact plans to execute, and all of her expectations managed, this fluid and intuitive journey of surrendering to the universe and trusting I'm on the right path is an ongoing lesson and practice.

Right now, I'm just trying to have this experience. I'm trying to share my journey with the hope of being a catalyst for other women to change their own lives, so that they can follow their authentic path too. I believe that when more women start living with passion and purpose, following their true path, and stepping into their power, the world can't help but be changed for the positive.

I want to help them—and YOU—do it your own way. Consider this handbook your invitation to begin.

. . . .

Contents

....

Part 3: Healing

Part 4: A Sprinkle Of Magic

How To Use This Handbook

....

If you're anything like I used to be, you're probably reading this hoping I'm just going to lay it all out for you: "Here's How To Use This Book (i.e. change your life) in Ten Easy Steps". The bad news (but really, the good news!) for all you type-A Alpha Sisters is that you're not going to find any of that here. Growth, personal development, and forging your own path are not always linear processes—and they definitely can't be done by following a strict to-do list.

So here's how to use this handbook: however you damn well want to. Forwards, backwards, upside down, inside out, jumping around. You just pick it up off the shelf and follow your instincts. Maybe you scan the table of contents and one chapter jumps out at you immediately—that's your cue to start there. Maybe you want to dive headfirst into the (gorgeous, if I do say so myself) illustrations before taking on the rest of the content. Maybe you want to read it methodically, from beginning to end. Maybe you want to read it methodically from end to beginning. The point is, there's no right or wrong way to use it. (I mean, I guess the wrong way to use it would be *not* to use it, but if you've gotten this far you should really keep going—I've got some pretty great stuff in store for you.)

I hope this book feels like a chat with your best friend over coffee, or a casual lunch with your favorite mentor—something filled with short, easily-digestible bursts of encouragement, accompaniment, and helpful tips. At times, you might want to take a moment to meditate or journal about what you've read—contemplating your own point of view, checking in with your higher self, and considering how (or if) you want to integrate what you've just read into your own life. (And if you don't, that's okay too!)

The only rule is that there are no rules. Use this book as a way to guide you towards discovering your higher self, and then connecting with that self more deeply. Let it hang out alongside you as you navigate the wild, wonderful twists and turns of your own life. Follow where you intuition leads you.

Oh yeah, and sister? Don't forget to have a little fun along the way. (I know I did.)

. . . .

Part 1
Being An Alpha

BEING AN ALPHA vs. BEING A BITCH: 11 TENETS

1. AN ALPHA *KNOWS* SHE'S POWERFUL. A BITCH JUST PRETENDS TO KNOW IT.

2. AN ALPHA FEELS SECURE WITH HER PLACE IN THE WORLD. A BITCH FEELS INSECURE.

3. AN ALPHA DOESN'T GOSSIP. A BITCH LOVES TO GOSSIP.

4. AN ALPHA SUPPORTS OTHER WOMEN. A BITCH STABS THEM IN THE BACK.

5. AN ALPHA WILL STAND HER OWN GROUND. A BITCH HIDES FOR SAFETY.

6. AN ALPHA AVOIDS DRAMA. A BITCH THRIVES IN DRAMA.

7. AN ALPHA LOVES HERSELF. A BITCH LOATHES HERSELF.

8. AN ALPHA RESPECTS THE BOUNDARIES OF HERSELF AND OTHERS. A BITCH DOESN'T.

9. AN ALPHA IS A LEADER. A BITCH IS JUST A MEAN GIRL.

10. AN ALPHA IS GENEROUS. A BITCH ONLY TAKES FOR HERSELF.

11. AN ALPHA KNOWS THE POWER OF SISTERHOOD. A BITCH IS THREATENED BY SISTERHOOD.

Myths About Alpha Women

....

Every day, women around the world dare to step into their wildest dreams and the power of their authentic lives—and every day, the world changes a little bit more. But not everyone is in favor of changing the world. In fact, a lot of the social and political structures that run our world depend on women playing small, staying silent, and following the rules. It's in this place that we find dangerous myths being told about strong and powerful (aka Alpha) women.

In my own experience, whenever a woman is described as an Alpha, she's viewed as one of two stereotypes. The first is that Alpha Women can't work together. Put two or more Alphas together in a room and power struggles, jealousy, tempers, and emotional drama will flare. The second is that Alpha Women are "too much" and must be "broken" into compliance—otherwise, they're just bossy, scary, dictatorial, difficult to work with, hard to manage, and arrogant.

Who wants to be any of that? None of the stories I was first told about Alpha Women felt empowering, or even fair. And despite these negative myths that surround Alpha Women, I still identified as an Alpha myself. But I wanted to describe and understand myself as an Alpha differently. I wanted to be a boss (just not "bossy"), strong and confident, grounded, and secure enough in myself to support the other Alpha Sisters around me. I wanted to revise the definition of an "alpha," change the false narratives that surround strong women, and build a sisterhood (what became the Alpha Female Sisterhood) to empower and celebrate Alphas and all the magic we have to offer the world.

We are positive, strong, empowered, and high-performing female leaders. The myths about Alpha Women—the false and biased descriptions of us—actually describe bitches. And chances are, if you're reading this book, you're an Alpha. Or at the very least, you've started your journey towards becoming one.

. . . .

Don't Just Know Your Power, Claim Your Power

....

Many women, from their earliest years of life, were taught to deny, stifle, or hide their power in favor of being "nice," getting along with others, and not being "too much." We discover we're smarter, harder workers, and more talented, gifted, and passionate than some of the people around us—but wind up keeping our skills and gifts to ourselves. (Seriously, how many of us know that we are The Shit, but just feel guilty admitting it?)

Too many of us are afraid to claim our power, celebrate our talents, and show up to our lives with our skills on full display. Instead, we downplay our power, avoid the spotlight, or even take on demeaning tasks in order to please other people or gain acceptance. Sometimes, women are afraid to claim their power for fear of failure or being rejected. (Sometimes women even fear success—and the life changes that come with it!) And too often, this behavior earns us acceptance and validation from society—after all, we're following the rules.

But here's the thing about fear: it gets you nowhere. Fear keeps you stuck, creatively blocked, financially trapped, emotionally suffocated, and in a place of zero growth—personally and professionally. (Not to mention fear is totally boring! You know what's *not* totally boring? All those crazy cool talents you have. We want to see some of those.) Being an Alpha means that we need to get a bit more courageous; to take ourselves one step further, beyond just knowing our power. We can't just stop at knowing our powers—we have to *claim* them too.

Once you know in your heart that you're smart, talented, really good at what you do, and super passionate about it, it's time to claim that! Recognize your power and then let others know about it too. Start to share with everyone else the truths you've known about yourself all along. You show up to your life, you take action, you create something new, you choose to make a difference. And ultimately, you live your purpose—all by showing up, sharing your voice, going after the things you want and deserve, taking the lead, and stepping up in a big way.

Sounds a little scary, right? (But also, pretty exciting.) The thing is, you don't have to grab a ladder and shout your talents from the rooftop right outta the gate—although, if you want to, I will be the first Alpha Sister to cheer you on. There are great ways to get in the habit of claiming your power without putting it *all* out there, all at once. Maybe you start by finding a fellow Alpha Sister and sharing your passion with her—and she'll be there to hold you accountable when it's time to execute those big plans of yours. Maybe you start with some self-affirmations—and we've got some great suggestions for celebrating your awesomeness later on in this book. Maybe you write down ten things you love about yourself every day before you head out the door to work.

Whatever it is that starts you on the road to claiming your power, know that it's only by being your authentic self, celebrating your talents, and living your purpose that you're going to realize the fullness of all of your dreams—and sister, you totally deserve that.

....

Trust Your Intuition

....

Follow your gut, tune into your instincts, trust your intuition—these are not always messages that women are given. Instead, we're taught to use logic and analysis, demand proof, question our instincts, and second guess our intuition. But being connected to our intuition—and trusting the cues it sends us—can be life-changing. That's because the deepest, most divine messages the universe will ever send us come through intuition. And your intuition? As an Alpha Woman, that's your superpower.

Allowing your intuition to guide you in your daily life, your relationships, and your business is not just for "woo" people—it's for *everybody*. Sometimes people tell me they don't connect with intuitive stuff because they have more "analytical minds." Awesome, I have an analytical mind too. But what if tapping into that intuitive side of your mind is exactly what you need to work at your fullest potential? Tapping into the intuitive side isn't about replacing or merely improving the analytical side of your brain; rather, it's about getting full use of both. Consider how amazing and magical you could become if both the analytical and intuitive sides of your mind were wide open and working together? In fact, you can think of your intuition as your very own, personal "easy" button—one located in your heart center, that gives you "yes" or "no" directions towards making the right decisions.

Consider this formula: the logical thinking mind + the intuitive feeling heart + focused aligned action = Magic! And don't we all want a little more magic in our work and lives?

As high-achieving women, tapping into our constantly thinking, judging, and logic-driven mind is easy. But what many of us need to work on is learning how to feel our way into the messages coming from our intuition. Think about the last time you truly felt you *knew* something; maybe you didn't know why you knew it, or where your instinct was coming from, but nonetheless you were filled with a deep, clear knowing. That's your intuition— and it's only by following it that you'll begin to take steps towards living your most genuine, authentic, aligned life.

If you've been disconnected from your intuition, it might be challenging to tap into it at first—and even more challenging to trust it when it does clue you into where the universe is directing you. It definitely takes practice. You might have to start small— simply by paying attention. Intuition is a sensory experience—it's your body, mind, and soul working together to guide you towards (or even away from) something.

It's also important to get quiet—try to silence any "monkey mind" and listen to what is going on underneath all the chatter.

Judgmental thoughts, negative feelings, fears of criticism—these are all things that work against your intuition, and make it harder to tune into your truest self.

Finally, you have to start taking clear action on the cues from your intuition. When you experience that gut feeling, follow it. When your instincts clue you into something, listen to them. When your intuition sends you a message, trust it. And then let it guide you to whatever the universe has in store for you next.

....

Pick Your Battles

....

One of the biggest lessons for us Alpha Sisters is to learn how to pick our battles, and to realize that not every fight is our fight. (I know, I know—easier said than done.) When you're a passionate and strong personality people often expect you to lead them in their battles to victory (at home; at the office; at the coffee shop; at the restaurant and the dry cleaners too!).

What this means is that, all too often, Alpha Sisters get trapped in fights that aren't ours. Nobody knows this feeling better than me. Back when I was in my twenties, I thought everything was a battle. I always felt the need to prove everyone wrong and be the smartest, savviest person in the room. (Basically, I was trying way, WAY too hard.) But all of that only stemmed from my own insecurity, my judgment of myself and others, and my feeling that I was better than others—or that I had to be. I was putting out a ton of low-vibration-unhealthy-mindset-negative-energy shit. I found myself building a reputation as someone who was good at what she did, but who was not fun to work with. (And let's be honest, don't we all want to be fun to work with?)

Eventually, I learned how to pick my battles. But more importantly I fought my battles in ways that stayed true to my core values. Of course, I also tried to focus on being fair and supportive, creating a team environment, owning my responsibilities instead of placing blame on others, and focusing on solutions not problems—the kind of stuff we *all* want to be good at, especially in the workplace. And you know what? My professional life transformed.

Another way to think about this is by looking at the animal kingdom. Within a pack of wolves—another species that recognizes Alpha Women—the wolfpack leader (the Alpha) doesn't often engage in battle herself. She has more important things to do. These Alphas only fight when it's important for the survival of themselves or their wolfpack. And when an Alpha wolf does fight, she fights to the death.

Be like the Alpha wolf: know when a fight is your fight, and when it's not.

Think that's easier said than done? Think again. The key is to know what your nonnegotiables are. Basically, you have to ask yourself: What are your core values? What is so important to you that you'd fight to the death for it? But for the most part, resist the temptation to fight other people's battles—and in your own battles, always look for the potential for a peaceful resolution. Remember: be like the Alpha wolf.

....

How To Handle Rivalry

....

Let's take a minute to talk about Alpha rivalry. If you've ever experienced it, you're definitely not alone. This rivalry between women—feeling the need to compare, or wondering why one thing happens to a fellow Alpha Sister but not you—exists not because there's something inherently competitive or jealous about Alpha Women; it exists because of the pressures society places on women and the ways we're often pitted against ourselves and each other.

In my own journey, I encountered so many messages to "watch my back" when it came to other women. In my personal life, my mom taught me to always be conscious of introducing my boyfriends to my best friends, because they might "steal" them. In my professional life, I was taught to keep my distance from other capable women and focus on competing with them for the spotlight (because in the corporate world, there was usually just ONE opportunity for a woman to shine—if there was any at all—and the idea was that other women would try to undermine, compete with, or sabotage me). But in hindsight, I feel like this messaging was nothing more than some totally fucked-up way the patriarchy tries to keep women from becoming powerful on our own. There is strength in numbers—and the more women who lead, the more powerful we all are.

Very often, these feelings of rivalry or competition are rooted in a lack mindset—the idea that there simply isn't enough (money, clients, opportunities, success) to go around; that once one woman achieves something awesome, then that awesomeness is gone for the rest of us, forever. It can also originate in our own feelings of personal insecurity and inadequacy—and rather than showing us areas where we need to improve, it highlights how we can work harder to celebrate, love, and accept ourselves.

Here's the thing: it's both natural and okay to experience negative emotions—like jealousy—when comparing yourself to another Alpha Sister. When you do have these feelings, the best thing to do is to notice and acknowledge them; don't repress and ignore your feelings or scold yourself for your thoughts. In these moments, treat yourself like would treat your best friend: remind yourself of all the ways you're *already* amazing; recall moments when the universe offered you abundance; find space to celebrate the success of a fellow sister.

When I finally changed my views about my fellow Alpha Sisters and developed the mindset that we can actually be a sisterhood of strong, capable women who are genuinely interested in rising together, magical things happened. Suddenly, more and more women began showing up for me in my life, forming a sisterhood where we started creating bigger impacts and more successes for ourselves and one another.

Imagine what it would be like if we all fully embraced the concept of abundance—believing that there's enough good to go around and opening ourselves up to the opportunities the universe wants to send our way so we could, in turn, celebrate the successes of our sisters. (aka "when she rises, we all rise!") At the same time, by cultivating an abundance mindset we also become secure and loving in our own lives—showing up, believing in ourselves and championing our successes, while also not being afraid to ask for help when we need it. (And then believing we're deserving of the help that comes!)

So, Alpha Sisters, let's commit to transcend the narratives of the "catty woman" and rewrite the stories about female rivalry. Let's transform them into a path to collective power instead. Let's be courageous enough to form a sisterhood that supports all of us. Let's recognize that by celebrating each other's accomplishments, saving room for one another at the table, and helping each other rise, we Alphas will create some real, badass magic in the world.

. . . .

Dismantle The Patriarchy:
Burn Your Fire, Baby

....

Let's just be honest: the patriarchy is the worst. There is no bigger enemy to feminism, empowered women, and women embodying their most authentic selves than the patriarchy. It is a strong, powerful enemy—one that has laid the foundation for our culture and weaved itself through thousands of years of our history. As an Alpha Sister, you have a responsibility to burn your fire against the patriarchy.

But what does that actually mean? After all, everyone's fire looks and feels different. Some fires are fast burning, like the hot flames of activism, fiery voices against the patriarchy. Others are more slow burning—but once they get going, they burn steadily. Some fires are like a secret candlelight, burning quietly underground.

Part of being an Alpha Sister is daring to burn your fire against the patriarchy. But equally important is understanding and respecting the fires of the others too. You might be an outdoor bonfire, crackling loudly against the patriarchy while your fellow Sister's fire is a candle burning by an open window. This doesn't mean you're better, stronger, or more committed than her. We need as many fires as we can get to burn against the forces that oppose us.

When it comes to dismantling the patriarchy, we can't afford to judge one another or fight amongst ourselves. *Every* fire burned against the patriarchy plays a critical role, and we need them all. It is your right to choose how you wish to burn. But let your flame burn, Sister; let that flame burn.

. . . .

On Being Childfree By Choice

....

Let me start off by saying: few things are more fraught for a woman than the Motherhood conversation. There are all sorts of feelings and opinions at play when it comes to the choice to mother, the choice NOT to mother, the inability to mother when you want to, or the decision to mother when you weren't really planning (oops!) to do so in the first place. I've experienced plenty of judgment and criticism from both men and women for my own choices too, notably shock or scorn when they realize I'm childfree by choice. I've also encountered times where I've been told I don't understand something because I'm not a mother. (True, but dismissive). But here's something I know: making a decision about your life, or about how to *share* your life, based on the fear of how others will respond is not what Alpha Sisters do. I hope this empowers any woman who identifies as a member of the hyper-minority of women choosing to be childfree—and loving it.

I have always felt that becoming a mother was not my thing. Even growing up, I never played with a doll or imagined having a traditional family. My childhood dreams and playtime fantasies included going on adventures and changing the world—without a toddler in tow. Sure, there was a period of time in my 20s and 30s when societal pressures and the expectations of men combined to create some angst around my desire not to follow the traditional path of motherhood. Looking back, I am so thankful that I managed to stay my course.

As a now-forty-something, I am thankful (honestly, every day) for a life that does not include motherhood. To me, motherhood feels like a powerful, thriving, massive, amazing, demanding, beautiful, and messy club. But it's not *my* club to join. And I believe, in my heart and my soul, that my choice to remain childfree has allowed me to be fully present and dedicated to my life's purpose and mission.

If you're childfree by choice, maybe struggling with how people in your life and culture understand your choice, here are some examples of why I personally love this path; maybe these will inspire and comfort you too:

★ I am free to make decisions and take opportunities that feel authentically right for me without having to weigh their impact on the happiness, life, or death of other humans that I love. It is easy to say yes.

★ I have total permission and freedom to be "selfish"—to live according to my own needs, wants, and purpose, exclusively.

★ Mom Guilt? What is that?

★ I am pretty immune to the "Mommy Wars" aka "Mom Judgments" aka that phenomenon that the minute a woman becomes a mother her life, body, and decisions suddenly become the subject of constant and relentless public debate. This form of insidious, toxic femininity is not something I have to worry about.

★ Quiet. Quiet home, quiet car, quiet mornings, quiet whenever and wherever I want. Just, quiet.

★ Traveling. For work, for fun, for love, for sisterhood, for growth, for learning, for inspiration. I travel. A lot.

★ My relationship with my partner continues to be about just two of us. We evolve, we connect, we grow, and we love each other for who we are, individually.

★ I have far fewer competing priorities when it comes to showing up for my friends, my clients, and everyone else in my life. I can be a present friend who is generous with my time, resources, and love.

★ I literally do not know what it is like to be responsible for another human being's survival, health, education, character, behavior, happiness, success, and various bodily fluids. I am free to fear less and worry less.

Need some more empowerment in your choice to remain childfree? Consider turning to the lives and work of these inspiring, magical childfree women: Oprah Winfrey, Gloria Steinem, Stevie Nicks, Dolly Parton, Betty White, Elizabeth Gilbert, Jane Austen, Diane Sawyer, Leslie Jones, Coco Chanel... and so many more.

. . . .

On Being An Alpha Mama

....

Now that we've tackled being childfree by choice, what about the Alpha Sisters who do choose motherhood? How do they strike that balance between career, family, and everything else we Alphas fill our wild, wonderful lives with? Can an Alpha Sister really "have it all"? (And by the way, what is "it all," anyway?)

I've called upon some of my fellow sisters—Alpha Mamas—to share their experiences and best advice.

"Your definition of success has to change. We don't live in a culture that supports our mothers, so we have to find a way to support ourselves. Find a tribe of mothers—mothers who are also balancing a career with a child/ children. Anyone who tells you to sleep when the baby sleeps hasn't tried to do what you're doing, so they are not your tribe right now. Accept that 95% of the time you will be choosing between your career and sleep. You'll think it will kill you, but it won't, and it's not forever. At the very least, motherhood forces you to get really clear, really quickly, about what you really love. And if you really love the work that you do, you'll find your own way to make it happen."
– Emily M.

"Trust your gut. No one will know your baby better than you. Try to not sweat the small stuff. [If you delivered vaginally] use the ice filled gloves postpartum, because your whole nether region will hurt. Breastfeeding takes a few weeks to be "natural," so find humor and give yourself grace."
– Jenny D.

"Treat yourself, ask for help, and it's ok to be imperfect."
– Monica B.

"Just when you think you've got things figured out or under control, it all changes! Flexibility is key as well as letting go of expectations (or any idea of perfection; it doesn't exist!). The more you try to control things, the harder it gets. Go easy on yourself."
– Jessica C.

"When you are planning your week, be sure to schedule time for your family and uninterrupted time for your kids, specifically. Prioritize it like any business appointment you might have: it helps manage the inevitable "mommy guilt" while letting them know they are your priority in a demonstrable way."
– Katie Z.

"One of the greatest gifts you can give your kids is to be happy yourself. Some of the most worrisome and sad moments of my life have been when I realized my parents weren't happy. So I fight for and defend my happiness fearlessly, not only for myself but for my children's sake."
– Anonymous

"Don't feel guilty if you don't enjoy every moment. It's parenting, not martyrdom. I was not a fan of the newborn stage and I finally let go of the guilt. People will always ask: "Don't you miss that?" Nope, sure don't, and I'm fine with it."
– Kristine W.

"Children are a gift from the universe in that they both reflect our deepest wounds and are also our greatest opportunity to heal. It is not our job to mold our children into the people they're meant to be; rather it is our job to help them unfold into the fullness of their being. In this selfless act of unconditional love, we experience forgiveness, healing, and hope all at once."
– Christina T.

....

"It may be tempting to make them your "mini-me" especially when you see a lot of similarities between you. Allow them to be their own self by giving them the space to explore and build their own style and personality."
– Jeannie S.

Cultivate Humility
(Sometimes You Don't Know Shit)

....

Let me tell you a little story: When I was in my early 20s and was a rising star in my career, I used to think I knew it all. I considered it my personal responsibility to show everyone around me how qualified, capable, talented, and intelligent I was—and specifically, how much better I was than others. If you ask me, all my thoughts were the brightest thoughts, all my ideas were the greatest ideas, all my accomplishments were the best accomplishments—and highlighting all the ways others weren't as competent or talented as I was became an essential part of my job. (Um, yes I was kinda a bitch.)

My attitude and behavior gave me the reputation of someone who was difficult to work with (and basically a huge pain in the ass.) Suddenly, I started experiencing challenges at work—all of which were a direct result of my behavior and how I treated others. Thankfully, I had a lot of great mentors who helped guide me towards a new way of seeing and doing things. On my own, I also grew from experiences where I'd failed or felt betrayed myself—times when my being so sure of myself turned out to be a bad idea, or instances when people I trusted didn't end up coming through for me. I learned to develop humility, to understand how to work on a team, and collaborate with others.

Some of my female mentors, in particular, taught me how to be an Alpha who shared the spotlight with other women, opened up seats at the table, and supported the voices of others. I learned that those times when they didn't speak up or hoard the limelight weren't because they didn't have the courage or weren't confident enough to do so—it was because they were mature, evolved, and knew that there were many ways to get a job done. Their ability to tap into their humility and their willingness to compromise their position and learn from each other actually provided *more* powerful opportunities to make impacts in the workplace (and the world.)

These lessons allowed me to become an even stronger leader and more effective in my work. Now, I know the value of many women's voices over a few; the strength of multiple perspectives in tackling one project or problem; the power of sharing the spotlight. Not only does humility make me a more effective leader, it also allows me opportunities to learn from the wisdom and experiences of others I might've missed out on if I'd been singularly focused on my own accomplishments and agenda.

It can be hard to find the balance between sharing and celebrating your hard-won strengths and talents, and approaching situations with humility. Don't get me wrong: we ladies definitely deserve to toot our own horns now and again! The key is to remember that you don't know everything (and sometimes, you honestly don't know shit) and it's OKAY that you don't know everything. When it's your time to shine, you will. And when it's time to share the spotlight with others, move on over sister!

....

11 Ways To Be Your Own #1 Advocate

....

When was the last time you realized you wanted something, felt you deserved it, and then went after it with everything you've got—even when "everything" meant literally having to *ask* for it? Whether at work, in relationships, or in the basic rhythms of daily life, being able to advocate for yourself is one of an Alpha's secret weapons. It's also something that can be super challenging to master—especially if you're used to feelings of shame around your desires, unworthiness around getting what you want, or fear of voicing what you need.

Shame, fear, and unworthiness are some of the most powerful limiting beliefs out there—and they create energetic blocks that feel nearly impossible to move past. The truth is, they all originate from a sense of believing that we're not enough: that we don't deserve what we're asking for, that we haven't earned it, and the fear of possible rejection if and when we finally do ask.

So how do we silence that inner critic who tells us we're not worthy of what we want and eliminate that feeling of guilt when we ask for what we want or just take it for ourselves? How do we move beyond our fears of criticism and rejection and learn to not only accept ourselves, but to advocate for ourselves as well?

1. **Practice cultivating an abundance mindset.** Believe the universe has enough for you and everyone else as well. It's easier to be your own advocate when you don't feel like you're taking opportunities or resources from others.

2. Check in with yourself—make sure what you're advocating for is in line with your beliefs, values, energy, and where you want your life to be going forward.

3. Set an intention around what you want. Before you ask your boss/spouse/friend/etc. for what you want, ask the universe to create space in your life for it and to prepare you to receive it.

4. Believe you deserve to not only advocate for yourself, but to get what you want as well. If you don't believe in your worthiness, nobody else will either.

5. Prepare as though you're going to receive everything that you're advocating for. The last thing you want to happen is to manifest what you desire, and then realize you're not ready for it.

6. Ask for what you want (and deserve!) clearly, directly, and with conviction.

7. Advocate big. Now is not the time to be conservative with your end goals. Take yourself seriously enough to dream big, and then advocate big.

8. Don't take the first "no" for an answer. Be persistent. Know your worth and don't give up until that worth is matched in returns.

9. Consider alternatives. Still not getting what you want, even after advocating for yourself like a champ? Then it might be time to move on—from a job, from a relationship, from anything in your life that isn't offering a return on your investment of energy, expertise, time, or money.

10. Don't take rejection as a reflection of your worth! Think of rejection as a guiding nudge from the universe, sending you (and your badass self-advocating skills) in a different direction. Once you realize what that direction is, advocate for yourself there!

11. Remind yourself what a powerful practice it is to be able to advocate for yourself—and celebrate yourself when you do!

By believing that we are enough, we invite ourselves to show up in the world exactly as we are and to honor the worth of our being. When this happens—when we become our own advocates—all kinds of magic is possible! It just starts with believing in our worthiness, exactly as we are, and then daring to be our own #1 advocates.

....

"Fuck It, I'm Awesome" And Other Affirmations

....

Let's face it: as much as we'd all like to be our own personal round-the-clock cheerleaders, we're human; and that means that sometimes, we get stuck in some pretty negative spirals. Whether we're struggling with feelings of not being good enough or are suffering from full-blown imposter syndrome (that pattern of total B.S. behavior that has you doubting your accomplishments and struggling with fears of suddenly being exposed as a fraud—which you're NOT!) the fact is that sometimes we all need a little help quieting that inner voice that tells us we're inadequate.

If you've found yourself thinking thoughts like "who am I to dream big and manifest what I want?" or "there are far more qualified people doing what I do so much better," then you definitely need a kickass mantra (or several) to help you snap out of it in a big way.

Lucky for you, I'm surrounded by badass women all day, every day, many of whom are more than happy to share their go-to mantras with you—and who know firsthand that this shit really works.

The practice of mantra is so effective because by speaking the language of an affirmation or holding a mantra in our mind, we're not just telling ourselves a series of words, but also allowing ourselves to enter the energetic vibrations of those words. The energy of a mantra enters not only the conscious mind, but the unconscious mind as well—influencing all aspects of yourself, even those you might not consciously be aware of. The right mantra will raise your vibration, shift your energy, and move you from a space of insecurity into one of courage; a space of reluctance into one of vitality. The most important part of any mantra practice is that when you engage with the words, your focus is on feeling the energy and emotions of those words in your body. Don't just repeat an affirmation or mantra with your mouth—feel the awesomeness in every cell of your being, as you're saying it. That's when you'll realize the practice is truly working.

Below are some of the sassy, powerful, and effective mantras that have been collected from the Alpha Female Sisterhood, all great for snapping you out of a negative mindset and releasing you from a spiral of self-judgment. Plus, there's some space at the end to include a few favorite mantras of your own.

"Fuck It, I'm Awesome." – Seo

"I am Motherfucking Queen." – Weslie

"I am the Shit." – Meriel

"I'm the Light." – Stacy

"I'm Magic." – Natasha

. . . .

Part 2
Playing Big

Manifesting: Step by Step Process (Otherwise Known As "Ordering Your Pizza")

....

You might want to manifest yourself a snack before diving into this lesson—because I've got a pizza metaphor that's guaranteed to help you in your quest toward manifestation mastery. The caveat: it might also make you a little hungry. Let's get to it.

When I talk about manifesting—what I often refer to as "ordering your pizza"—I want you to imagine that the universe is kind of like a restaurant (in this case, your favorite pizza parlor). Here, "ordering your pizza" is the key to manifesting whatever you desire, courtesy of the universe.

Let's imagine you've just arrived at a restaurant: you didn't eat breakfast this morning, you had a busy day, and you're hungry. You're not just hungry, you're ravenous. You'd eat the napkins, if they'd let you. But you don't just show up to a restaurant, sit down at a table, and say: "I want food, I need food, bring me food." (I mean, maybe *some* people do this... but they probably don't end up getting the exact food they want very often.) The point is, the restaurant (the universe) will bring you *something*. But it's probably not going to be what you really want.

So here you are, hanging out at your favorite pizza joint, getting ready to place your order. You want to make sure the pizza you get is the pizza you want, right? And with so many options—different types of crusts and sauces, a variety of cheeses, countless toppings—you have to be specific. And that, pizza lovers, is basically what manifesting is: it's how you order your pizza. The more specific and detailed you are when you order, the better the chances are that you're going to get the pizza you want. (And at the end of the day, don't we all really just want to get the pizza that we ordered?)

That's the first step to manifesting: placing your order with detail and specificity. But that's not quite all there is to it. You also have to make sure you pay for your order—in other words, once you've clearly expressed what you want, you need to take an aligned action step to ensure you're doing your part in making your manifestation happen. This action should feel clear and natural, it shouldn't be especially challenging or strenuous, but you do need to put forth *some* effort in helping the universe manifest your desires. Basically, be sure you're doing your part too.

Back at the pizza parlor, you're sitting at your table, maybe you're chatting with your friends. You've just placed your order and you're waiting for the pizza to arrive. I don't know about you, but when I order a pizza, I do not spend the next twenty minutes worrying about whether or not my pizza is being made correctly. You don't place your order and then walk back into the kitchen to see if the restaurant is making your pizza to your specifications—tossing your crust perfectly, adding the correct sauce—do you? No! You don't stress about how they're making your pizza, you just trust that they're doing it.

That's the exact mindset you want to bring into your manifesting. Once you place your order to the universe, you don't worry about how the universe is going to make it happen. You just wait for your "pizza" to arrive.

To be fair, this is where a lot of people get stuck in their manifesting practice. It's tempting to start wondering about what you're hoping to manifest: will it happen, when will it happen, how will it happen, all the ways it might not actually happen at all, how challenging things might become if it *does* happen. But that's not our job. That's the job of the universe. Your only job, in fact, when it comes to manifesting (or ordering a pizza, for that matter) is to place the order, pay for the order—take clear action that supports the arrival of your order—and then trust the universe will provide.

Now, back at the restaurant, your food has just arrived, and the pizza is perfect. What's the first thing you do? You say "Thank you," of course! Then you get down to the business of eating and enjoying. But expressing that gratitude is key. And chances are, the restaurant will respond in kind: "Well, aren't you a wonderful customer," they'll say. "You should keep coming here! I'll always make your favorite pizza. Or pasta! Or steak!" The universe operates in the same way.

But let's say your pizza isn't perfect. Maybe there was a miscommunication when you ordered or an error in the kitchen. It's still important to express gratitude. Sure, you can explain that you actually wanted something different— but do so through a spirit of understanding and thankfulness. (Basically, the key is that you not become a huge asshole. We've all seen these kinds of people before and it's not a good vibration.) It's essential that whether the pizza—or whatever you've manifested from the universe—is perfect, not quite right, or totally wrong, you still express gratitude and create the right vibration so the universe can take the "pizza" back and make it right.

When it comes to manifesting, all you've got to do is show up, place your order, pay for it, let go of any worries while you're waiting for your order to arrive, and then find gratitude when it comes.

....

MANIFESTING
OR
"ORDERING YOUR PIZZA"

STEP ONE — **ASK** THE UNIVERSE FOR WHAT YOU WANT.

HEALTHY RELATIONSHIP

FLUFFY DOG

MAY I ORDER ONE LARGE PIZZA WITH A PROMOTION AND EXTRA FREE TIME.

BIG PROMOTION

FREE TIME WITH FAMILY & FRIENDS

HOUSE WITH A FENCED YARD

STEP TWO — TAKE CLEAR **ACTION**.

STEP THREE

TRUST THE UNIVERSE WILL PROVIDE.

STEP FOUR

RECEIVE WITH GRATITUDE.

9 Ways You Could Be Blocking Your Manifestation Mojo

....

So now that you know everything there is to know about "ordering your pizza"—and might be feeling totally jazzed about placing your next order to the universe—it's a great time to explore a few reasons why manifesting might not have worked out for you in the past, and tackle any blocks that might be getting in your way: once and for all.

1. **You want something that's not in alignment.** Basically, you might be attempting to manifest an arbitrary goal or intention that doesn't exactly line up with where you're at in your life. You want to be clear on why you're asking for exactly what you're asking for (and you should actually have a good reason—it's time to get real with yourself, Sister!).

2. **Your conscious mind and your subconscious mind are in conflict.** Confused? Stick with me a moment. When your conscious mind and your subconscious mind are in conflict, this is usually when you say you want something, but

your heart and soul really aren't in it. Maybe you have an underlying fear of failure, or a limiting belief that is holding you back; these are things you'll need to squash, ASAP. Now is a great time to take a meditation class or schedule an appointment with your favorite acupuncturist.

3. **You are playing small, when you should be dreaming big.** In other words, you're intentionally limiting yourself. (So, if you're ordering your pizza, you are ordering a small, thin-crust pizza without many toppings—even though you actually want that fully-loaded deep dish.) Maybe you're struggling with a lack mindset, feelings of guilt, or the sense that what you want isn't all that realistic. In that case: turn to gratitude. All of these feelings can be resolved by recognizing what abundance is already in your life, and freeing yourself to make room for more of it. (Because you deserve it, girl!)

4. **You are trying too hard.** You've gone from motivated to totally obsessed. (Take a breath, it happens to the best of us.) If you're constantly studying manifestation, learning different techniques, and totally over-thinking it, this might be the block you're struggling with. You've gotta sit back, have faith in yourself, and let the universe do its work.

5. **You are being too specific.** If you're too attached to the "how" of manifesting—how what you've manifested is going to happen, how it might not happen—then the universe doesn't have the space to do what it needs to do, to bring you want you want. This is a total bummer. Your only job now is to let go and let the universe take over. Basically,

you've got to relinquish some of your control and start practicing flexibility. (I know, I know—easier said than done. But I believe in you!)

6. **You, uh, forgot to take action.** So, you've started the process with the right intention... now what? If you're waiting for someone else to do all the heavy lifting, it's time to get off your butt and kick some—because you can speak your wishes to the universe all day, but zero action still equals zero results. It's time to get up, find a friend who will hold you accountable, and then start taking real steps to make it happen.

7. **You're not open to receiving.** Aka you're missing out on all the joy. While there's nothing wrong with paying the goodness in your life forward, if you're constantly trying to give back and even the scales every time something good happens to you, the universe notices. Instead of focusing on giving back what you've manifested the moment you receive it, send it a little "thank you" energy to the universe instead by enjoying what you have received—or next time the universe might just stand you up.

8. **You haven't created enough space.** It's time to declutter: your calendar, you to-do list, your relationships, maybe even some of your material stuff. No matter how mindfully you've manifested, the universe just doesn't have the space to bring you what you want. Start by creating physical space (yeah, actually tidying up your home). Once your physical space opens up, your energetic and spiritual space will follow: establishing room for new, positive energy in your life (and whatever it is you've manifested!).

9. You are ignoring the signs and guidance from the universe. Uh hello: you're not paying attention, here! The universe is clearly trying to tell you something, but you've gotten so preoccupied by the process of manifesting that you've totally tuned out. Turn to a practice that'll tune you into the universe and the signs it's sending your way: meditation, pulling tarot cards, free writing or dream journaling—anything that draws you closer to your intuition.

....

About FEAR

....

If you're someone who struggles with fear, then you know what an absolute monster it can be—halting your goals, stalling your plans, crushing your ambition, and making you question *everything*. I recently heard that fear ("FEAR") can be explained as False Expectations Appearing Real. Which is to say: far too often our fears are not rooted in reality or probability, but simply *feel* real—and they're doing nothing but holding us back. The fact is, we have no idea whether our fears will manifest into a reality; and in the meantime, they're keeping us from playing big, taking action, and following our dreams.

But still… the thing about fear is that it's always going to be there in one way or another. Fear is essentially the ego part of ourselves trying to keep us safe from risk, loss, and harm (and yeah, sometimes just plain ol' embarrassment). We cannot eliminate fear—at least, not entirely. But neither should we allow fear to debilitate us and prevent us from moving forward in our goals, dreams, and lives.

Ask yourself this: what if you moved forward *with* fear? What if you thought of fear less like a deadly monster hiding under your bed, and more like a sort-of annoying but well-meaning older sibling who follows you around filled with warnings (that you wave off and mostly ignore)? What if you said to yourself: *sure, I might be scared shitless right now, but I'm just going to do this anyway?* What if you did big things and just brought your fear along for the ride?

If you're someone who finds herself contemplating the extremes—so much so, that you struggle to stay present or to take action (e.g.: "my business will go bankrupt if I take this risk; or "if I leave my partner I will never find anyone else")—then it's time to dig into your fear, recognize it for what it is, and then barrel right on past it. Salute your fear as you pass by it on your way to doing that wild, wonderful thing you've been dreaming of.

The following prompts are designed to walk you through your fears, step-by-step, so we can find more clarity in what's really holding us back. Sometimes you may find that the fear we think we have isn't really the real reason we're holding ourselves back, but something else.

Is my feared outcome an absolute certainty?

_____

_____

_____

_____

What is the ultimate consequence that I fear? (What's the worst that could happen?)

_____

_____

_____

_____

What's the inner voice that runs in the background when I am feeling this fear? (Hint: it usually starts with "I...")

_____

_____

_____

_____

Is my feared outcome a realistic or probable one, and is there any evidence that supports this? (Hint: probably not.)

_____

_____

_____

_____

Let's play devil's advocate: if my fears actually do come true, what actions will I take to resolve them?

_____

_____

_____

_____

What evidence supports the idea that my fears won't come true?

_____

_____

_____

_____

....

Surrendering vs. Controlling

. . . .

As a recovering "control freak," the battle between control and surrender is one I'm *definitely* familiar with. Throughout all those years of my life, when I was just waiting for the other shoe to drop, so to speak, I used control as a way to manage my anxiety and fear of failure—thinking that if I could only control every single aspect of my life and my work, I could prevent any discomfort or suffering. (Spoiler alert: it didn't.)

Once I began my own spiritual and personal development journey—through life coaching, working on my mindsets and limiting beliefs, and learning to trust in the universe—I realized that I had only created more discomfort, anxiety, and suffering in my life by trying to control everything and everyone.

But as soon as I surrendered control and began believing that the universe would guide and take care of me, (and, honestly, also setting the intention to "let the other shoe drop" occasionally— and then realizing I could actually pick it back up!) I discovered the world wasn't going to collapse around me and that some stuff just really isn't that big of a deal. This was a hugely empowering revelation—one that taught me about the courage it really takes to place your trust in the universe.

Now, I consciously work on surrendering to the flow of the universe and trusting that the universe will both guide and take care of me—and it always, *always* does. And would you believe it: I manifest so much more success, magic, joy, and new experiences when I live this way!

There are plenty of ways to start a "surrender practice" of your own—connecting to nature, meditating, practicing yoga, tapping into your intuition, utilizing affirmations, starting a gratitude practice, visualizing yourself as one with the universe and all its wild plans, and more. Start with one that speaks most clearly to you and let the universe guide you from there.

....

Understand Your Money Mindset and Create Space for Abundance

....

If there's one thing Alpha Sisters know how to do in this world, it's hustle. But just because we've got the goods to financially support ourselves doesn't mean we badass boss babes don't have some totally unhealthy hang-ups around money. That's right, I'm talking about your money mindset—and how that money mindset can help or hinder your ability to create abundance.

But before we dive too deep, you might be wondering: what are my beliefs around money, anyway? It's probably not something you think about often, but once you do you'll be shocked at how subtle (but deeply-ingrained) money beliefs can be, to influence your *entire* life.

Think about what core money beliefs you might have: what does money represent to you? What beliefs are self-limiting? Where do your beliefs come from? And hey, who even taught you this garbage, anyway? What kind of relationships did your parents or other childhood influences have with money?

Try this simple exercise by completing the following sentences:

1. Money is

_____

_____

_____

2. Money means

_____

_____

_____

3. In my life, money represents

_____

_____

_____

4. When I hear the words wealth and abundance, I think

_____

_____

_____

5. When I hear the words poverty and lack, I think

See! There's so much more going on with your money mindset than you realized—right?

But Alpha Sister, know you're not alone. Money mindset blocks are all too typical. The good news is, now that you're aware of what yours look like, you can start to work through them and move past them.

Here are 5 of the most common money mindset blocks:

1. Lack Mindset: the belief that there's not enough to go around or that someone else's gain is your loss

2. Fear of Money: the belief that money is evil, wealth and prosperity is bad, or that wanting money is shameful

3. Struggle Mindset: the belief that you get rewarded with money only after hard work, struggle, and suffering

4. Conflicted Self-Worth: the belief that you must constantly prove your worth or deserve money by working and earning constantly

5. Punishment Mindset: the practice of focusing only on lack or fear of not enough as a way to motivate self

When you get stuck in any of these mindsets, not only does your health and spiritual wellbeing suffer, your financial life actually suffers too—causing you to constantly stress about money, fixate on the fear of losing money, make fear-based decisions about your finances, resent others who seem financially secure, and actually spend *more* money on things you don't even need. (Counterintuitive, I know—but that's how messy these money mindsets can be!) The key is to transform whatever money mindset you're working from into one of prosperity, abundance, and gratitude.

Here are a few ways to start to transform your money mindset:

1. Start a gratitude practice—whether you're writing what you're thankful for down in a journal or simply starting or ending your day by voicing your gratitude aloud (and yeah, I'm talking EVERY DAY), it's impossible to stay in an unhealthy money mindset when you're drawing your awareness to everything you're grateful for.

2. Set aside time each day for affirmations or meditation. (Pro tip: there are some great money mindset affirmations for you to try in the next chapter.) Use this time to remind yourself of everything you are doing right, recognize thought patterns that are rooted in fear rather than facts, and begin to shift your energy away from dysfunction.

3. Pay it forward by giving back to people who don't have as much as you do. They key is to give generously within your means and with intention—maybe this is money, resources, services, advice, or time. Giving to others will actually help remind you of all the abundance you do enjoy.

The point is, all of us, at some point, will struggle with unhealthy money mindsets. But it's not until you face those mindsets head-on and shift your energy from one of fear or lack to one of prosperity that you'll start to transform your relationship with money. Once you recognize that the universe is abundant and there is always enough, you'll start manifesting the wealth and success you desire and deserve, too.

....

Heal Your Money Mindset Through The Chakras

....

Now that you have a better understanding of your money mindset (the healthy, the unhealthy, and everything in between), and how it impacts your ability to manifest abundance in your life, it's time to do some of the hard work of healing. Below you'll find a series of chakra-inspired affirmations designed to bring your attention to the places in your body that are intimately connected to your money mindset—sending breath, healing vibes, and abundance energy there.

Since each chakra is centered in a different part of the body and focused on a different feeling or idea, you might not need all of these affirmations, all of the time. (But if you do, that's okay too.) Just begin with the one that speaks to you and what you're hoping to achieve in your money mindset.

1. Root Chakra (Red)
If your challenge is feeling safe and supported in your right to take up space in this world—in your right to not only financially survive, but to *thrive*—the root chakra is where you want to turn.

Drawing your energy to the base of your spine, try repeating these words: "I deserve to take up space in this world. I deserve to thrive and feel secure in my ability to manifest abundance. I say 'no' to my fears about money."

2. Sacral Chakra (Orange)

Your sacral chakra, located in your lower belly, is basically your pleasure center—not only is it the space where your sensuality derives from, but it's also where you'll feel the joy, freedom, and excitement of creating abundance in your life. If you've noticed your relationship with money isn't an especially joyful one, try this affirmation: "I am releasing any feelings of guilt about money and wealth. I release all past trauma around financial issues. I forgive past financial mistakes I've made. I'm ready to move forward with joyful and freeing energy."

3. Solar Plexus (Yellow)

The solar plexus—located right in the center of your body—is the space where you hold confidence, empowerment, and self-worth. (Or, if you struggle with those feelings, it's the place you want to send some healing energy, now!) Breathing deeply into your solar plexus, say: "I am healing the shame and judgment that surrounds my financial situation. I am healing any wounds I hold regarding the impact of others on my finances. I am confident, empowered, worthy, and strong."

4. Heart Chakra (Green)

It won't surprise you to know that your heart chakra is where you hold love in your body: love for yourself, for others, and—when it comes to your money mindset—a balanced and healthy relationship with money. If you struggle with guilt, sadness, an inability to forgive, or even a rejection of money, this is the chakra to turn to. Sending energy into your heart space, tell yourself: "I am healing my sadness and grief around money. I forgive my past financial mistakes, and love myself enough to embrace money, abundance, and my ability to create healthy financial boundaries."

5. Throat Chakra (Blue)
Your throat chakra is your communication center, where you speak your truth to the world. If you struggle with clearly communicating your wants and needs, especially around money—asking for things can be hard!—this is the chakra to draw your attention to. Breathe directly into your throat and try to notice if there is any blockage or resistance there. As you breathe, repeat to yourself: "I am healing any lies or dishonesty I have within my money beliefs. I am healing any untruths I may have expressed about my wants, needs, or goals. I will be honest about my financial situation and communicate my needs in healthy and productive ways."

6. Third Eye (Indigo)
If your main struggle is finding the clarity, inspiration, and vision for creating the abundance you desire, then you might want to check in with your third eye chakra. As you send energy to the space between your eyebrows, say: "I am healing any uncertainty, creative blocks, illusions, and doubts that I have about money. I believe I can create the abundant future I desire."

7. Crown Chakra (Purple)

If you're ready to go directly to the source—your badass, abundance-manifesting life source, the crown chakra is the space for you. Drawing your energy to the crown of your head, try repeating this: "I open myself up to divine spiritual energy, I am ready to create a life of abundance and wealth. I release any attachment I feel to money, instead I embrace trusting and surrendering to the universe fully, in order to create the abundant life I desire."

Finally, invite yourself to move forward with confidence and gratitude. Try repeating these affirmations:

"I am ABUNDANT."

"I am PROTECTED."

"I am LOVED."

"Thank you, UNIVERSE.
Thank you, MOTHER EARTH."

. . . .

YOUR CHAKRAS

7. CROWN—
SPIRITUALITY,
CONNECTION TO UNIVERSE
"I CONNECT"

6. THIRD EYE—
AWARENESS,
VISION "I SEE"

5. THROAT—
COMMUNICATION
"I SPEAK"

4. HEART—
LOVE, HEALING
"I LOVE"

3. SOLAR
PLEXUS—
WISDOM, POWER,
PURPOSE "I DO"

2. SACRAL—
SEXUALITY,
CREATIVITY,
EMOTIONS
"I FEEL"

1. ROOT—BASIC TRUST,
FOUNDATION
"I AM"

@sarahchoi.rocks

Know Your Energy: Identifying the Feminine and the Masculine

....

Think about the energy you bring into your work, your relationships, and your daily life. Are you very driven, always getting things done and looking forward to that next big goal? Or, do you find yourself less task-oriented and more go-with-the-flow? Do you lead with your heart rather than your brain? Maybe you fall somewhere in the middle.

These different, dynamic energies are known as our masculine energy and our feminine energy. Important to note is that they have nothing to do with whether or not you identify as male, female, or somewhere in between. Each of us contains both "masculine energy" ("doing" energy) and "feminine energy" ("receiving" energy). In fact, masculine and feminine energy exist everywhere; they're found not just in humans, but in animals and plants, minerals and magnetic poles, atomic particles— EVERYTHING. This energy absolutely influences how you exist in the world, so you're gonna want to get familiar with it and learn how to make it work for you.

Let's start by breaking down some of the basics.

You can recognize masculine energy through characteristics like:

★ Competitiveness, control
★ Making decisions with judgment and reason
★ Drive, hustle, striving, and pursuit
★ Focus on problem-solving
★ Being task-oriented

If you tend towards too much masculine energy, you might experience feelings of being stressed and overwhelmed. You may get things done effectively, yet feel uninspired and unfulfilled. You may feel like you've taken on too much work, insecure about your success, or frustrated with the results you're getting. You may be noticing a lack of support in your work. You might be creatively blocked or struggling to find a healthy work/life balance.

You may say things like: "I am working, working, and working, so why aren't things happening?"; "There is so much to do, I can't keep up"; "Why do others seem to manifest so much easier than me?"; or, "I am so frustrated with the lack of progress. I am working so hard!"

On the flip side, you can recognize feminine energy through characteristics like:

★ Being intuitive and receptive
★ Working collaboratively
★ Making decisions informed by feelings and emotions
★ Creativity
★ Nurturing others
★ Going with the flow or surrendering

If you're experiencing too much feminine energy, you might find that your efforts aren't manifesting the results you desire. You may have plenty of great ideas and inspiration but struggle to execute them. Maybe you are not experiencing results that align with your abilities and passion. You may feel frustrated or detached from your purpose, or experience a lack of focus or a clear direction. You might even feel like you're always doing more for others than you're doing for yourself.

You may say things like: "I am too overwhelmed with the actual step-by-step process to make things happen"; "I have so many great ideas, why can't I complete just one?"; "I need to focus and stop procrastinating"; or "I am really good at what I do—why can't I experience the success other people seem to be experiencing?"

Does any of this sound like you? Do you identify more with one side than the other?

All of these feelings result from an imbalance between your masculine and feminine energy—so if you identify with one energy more than the other, it's time to bring its complementary energy into your life. In the next chapter, I tell you how.

....

How To Balance The Feminine And The Masculine

....

So now that you know how to identify whether or not you experience an imbalance of masculine and feminine energy, what can you do about it? The good news is there are plenty of ways to balance your energy—and here I share some of my personal faves.

If you think you have an imbalance of too much masculine energy:

★ Start a gratitude practice: Everyday, write down 7–10 things you're thankful for and why you're thankful for them (that 'why' is super important). Also include 3 things about yourself that you are thankful for—because, duh, you're awesome, and also self-appreciation can be life changing.

★ Begin a meditation or mindfulness practice: Think of this as an opportunity to check in with yourself and ask what your heart is telling you. How are your intuition and instincts guiding you? What thoughts arise when you let the voice of your heart speak louder than the voice of your brain? (Did you even know your heart had a voice?) Try to refrain from over-thinking, over-analyzing and over-planning—I know, I know, easier said than done. But that's why we call it a *practice*. And with enough practice, you'll probably start noticing an increased sense of purpose growing within you, greater meaning, and more fulfillment in your work and life.

★ Sign up for a 21-Day Personal Development Detox: Take a break from all those books, articles, blogs, and podcasts about personal growth, success, hard work, or high-performance. It's time to clear the mind. Often, we don't realize how crowded our headspace is between the constant chatter of our inner critic to the prolific number of other voices (you know, the "experts" and "gurus") we cram in there too, all telling us what we "should" be doing. This is way too much noise.

★ Three words—play, rest, nurture: Since masculine energy is "doing energy," chances are if you have an excess of masculine energy you've been doing way too much—and it's time to balance this out. To do that, you need to cultivate intentional "do nothing" energy. This is going to be harder than you think. You might even feel anxious, guilty, or frustrated at first, but when you commit to incorporating more play, rest, and self-care into your life, you're guaranteed to notice a difference.

If you think you have an imbalance of too much feminine energy:

★ Try grounding: Grounding your energy is one of the most effective ways to stay focused and get things done. Consider trying a series of grounding yoga poses, like mountain pose, or standing in your bare feet outside, connecting physically to the earth.

★ "Pick Two": Having too many ideas or inspiration can be overwhelming. Ask yourself what are just TWO things that feel most aligned with your energy and joyful for you in this moment? Then work on those two ONLY. Only after accomplishing those two tasks should you allow yourself to move to the next new idea or opportunity.

★ Create accountability for yourself: Recruit an accountability partner, coach, or even an online community with whom you can share your goals (and who will hold you accountable). This can be an extremely powerful tool to help you get organized, focused, and take methodical, productive steps toward your goals. No accountability partner on hand? No problem. Try setting up notices (with alerts!) in your calendar or asking a friend or coworker to help keep you on task. Once you start to deliver more tangible results, you'll start to yield more tangible results as well—and that's the sweet spot where success and abundance start to flow into your life.

★ Game your reward system: Make focus and action a game for yourself (especially since trying to cultivate more masculine energy can feel rigid, painful, or frustrating). Avoid creating negative vibes by thinking of ways to make your tasks fun. For example, tell yourself that once you consistently take one action (from the two you've already selected above) for the next three weeks, you win a prize (e.g. that cool shirt you've had your eye on, a totally indulgent spa afternoon, a fancy meal at your favorite restaurant, etc.).

By nurturing the qualities of both energies, harmoniously, in your work, relationships, and life, you'll ultimately find greater focus, increased purpose, satisfying performance, abundance, a more natural flow, and an improved work/life balance. It's time to get after it, Sister.

....

Don't Be A "Fixer"

....

So far, we've spent a lot of time in this book talking about how to be there for our fellow sisters, how to support one another, and how to rise as a group. But there's definitely a line between supporting and "fixing"—and you're going to want to know where it is and what to do if you cross it.

A "fixer" is someone who dedicates herself to protecting others from discomfort, disappointment, or pain—even when *their* efforts cause discomfort, disappointment, and pain in themselves. Their intentions are usually always good and noble, and of course, there's nothing wrong with wanting to help change people's lives for the better. But when being a "fixer" comes at the expense of your own personal well-being and success, it winds up being destructive, leaving a trail of hurt, regret, or bitterness in its wake.

This is also an example of codependency. Codependency isn't necessarily about being needy; rather, it's when your own happiness or fulfillment relies upon your ability to make *other* people happy, thrive, or approve. When your feelings about yourself, your decisions, and the actions in your own life are dependent upon your ability to influence other people (or fix *their* problems), you are codependent.

At the heart of a "fixer" mentality is a whole lot of insecurity and probably some lack-mindset as well. When you consistently rank your own comfort, wellness, and happiness behind that of someone—or everyone!—around you, what you're really saying is: "I don't think I'm good enough on my own, so I'll 'fix' the people around me in order to alleviate my own insecurities and lack of self-worth." The truth? Not only is the person or people you're committed to "fixing" never going to change unless they do it on their own, they're going to bring you down with them in the process. And you deserve way better than that.

Here is another way we get into a fixer mentality. We think: "Focusing on myself and my own growth, healing, and transformation feels difficult, uncomfortable and scary, so instead I'm going to focus on others' problems because it's easier to shift my attention away from my own life." When we are "helping" or "fixing" other people, we escape blame for not paying attention to our own problems, right? This scenario is one of the most insidious and disempowering ways Alpha Sisters hold themselves back and play small. We need to stop this shit.

Ready to step out of the role of "fixer"? Here are four steps to get you started:

1. Recognize that you can't fix others. People only change when they're ready and willing, all on their own.

2. Be aware of your focus. Often the thing you're trying to "fix" in someone else is really something you've been avoiding fixing in yourself. Working on yourself and your own growth should be the priority over facilitating anyone else's.

3. Practice boundaries and find balance. You cannot be available 24/7. You cannot give all your money and other resources to others. You cannot continue to put your own dreams on the back burner while you try to help others achieve theirs. (You've heard the airplane analogy about putting your oxygen mask on first before helping those around you, right? That's exactly what we're talking about here.)

4. Set the intention to be an "advocate," a "friend," or a "supporter" instead of a "fixer." Language holds power and each word has its own, unique vibration. If you change the language, you change the energy.

The good news is, if you're someone that gets stuck in a "fixer" mentality, that means you're filled with giving, compassion, and generosity—all qualities that make Alpha Sisters the badass babes we are. It's just time to start being giving, compassionate, and generous to YOURSELF for a change.

....

Show Up For Your Sisterhood

....

It's time to let you in on the not-so-secret secret of true Alpha Woman power: behind every badass Alpha babe is a sisterhood of women supporting her. Friends, family, mentors, coaches, bosses—when one of us rises, we all rise. And as we do, it's Best Practice (and honestly, just way more fun) to bring a fellow sister or two along for the ride!

Showing up for your sisterhood not only fosters a sense of abundance, community, and compassion between Alphas, it works to dispel the myths surrounding the identity of Alpha Women. No one can accuse you of being competitive or difficult to work with if you're supporting those around you. Plus, there are tons of ways to show up for your sisterhood:

★ *attending another Alpha Sister's event, talk, or show*

★ *supporting your fellow Alphas by buying their goods or services (and then leaving a rave review if you love what they've got to offer!)*

★ *seeking out opportunities to be led by fellow women, or to lead in supportive ways*

★ *sharing your own top tips and tricks for success*

★ *sharing a fellow Alpha's success with others*

Personally, I love supporting my sisterhood—with energy, love, money and resources. It allows me to put my abundance mindset into practice, believing that what I put out into the universe will be returned back to me. (And guess what? It works!)

But what can we do if we find ourselves comparing our skills, opportunities, and resources with other Alphas around us? What happens if we start to feel self-critical or lacking and ask ourselves questions like: *"Why don't I have this when she does?"*; or thinking: *"Next time I'll do what she's doing."* When this happens, consider it a great opportunity to tune in to your inner voice and work through any mindset blocks you might discover. Then, practice being totally present for that sister and the work she's doing. How? Participate, attend, fund, encourage, promote and support. Ask yourself: *"How can I be fully present and stay authentic to my original intention of showing up for my fellow Alpha Sister?"* Presence and mindfulness in these instances can be extremely empowering, healing, and beneficial to our own growth.

....

⇒I ♥ MY⇐
SISTERHOOD

Resume vs. Eulogy:
How Do You Want To Live Your Life?

....

When I first came across the idea of "resume vs. eulogy" (i.e.: do you want to live your life in a way that will build your resume, or in a way that will leave behind a memorable eulogy?) it totally resonated with me. I realized that I had spent most of my life focused on building and living a resume. Suddenly, it was clear to me that if I died right at that very moment my eulogy would read a lot like a resume: the professional roles I'd filled, the jobs I'd had, the tasks I'd completed.

I thought to myself: *No way; I want my eulogy to be filled with stories about my relationships, lots of meaningful memories, the difference I made to the people around me, the community I built, and the impact I made on the world.* In that moment, I decided to start living my eulogy and not my resume.

If this idea resonates with you as well, the exercise below is a great way to get realigned with your authentic self and discover what it is you really want to live for.

Take 10 minutes to write your own eulogy. Begin with the words: "So and so passed away..." and then just let the pen guide you from there.

_____

_____

_____

_____

_____

_____

_____

_____

_____

_____

_____

_____

_____

_____

_____

Once you've completed the exercise, ask yourself: what things came up in your "eulogy" that you aren't yet living?

List some baby steps and first actions you can take to start integrating the elements of your eulogy into your daily life. What are a few things you want to start doing, right now? Is there anything you want to stop doing, instead? Get clear: how do you really want to live your life, starting today?

_____

_____

_____

_____

_____

_____

_____

_____

_____

_____

_____

_____

. . . .

Part 3
Healing

Authenticity, Self-Love, and Acceptance

....

Being "authentic" has become a buzzword—from those #nofilter selfies on social media to soul-bearing blog posts, letting your true self shine has never been so talked about before. And you've probably already heard more than you've ever wanted to hear about self-love and acceptance in this lifetime—am I right? These are super catchy buzzwords that seem to be everywhere these days, and for good reason.

But there can be something totally inauthentic about "authenticity," right? (In fact, so many of us are so used to filtering, sensoring, and monitoring ourselves, we don't even notice when we're doing it.) And no matter how much we might hear about it, we still struggle to both love and accept ourselves as we are. Yet, the most healing things you can do when trying to manifest the purposeful and joyful life you desire is greet the world with your most full self, practice self-love, and accept your authentic self.

It's been said that human beings become who they truly are by 8 years old. All your personality traits and preferences, your positive attributes and limiting beliefs, your fears and the voice of your inner critic—all things that will inform our lives for the rest of our lives—are pretty much established in early childhood, between birth and age 8. (No pressure.)

The thing is, it's during these years that the "conditioned self" is also formed—the self whose actions, thoughts, behaviors, and beliefs are influenced by the outside world and our experiences in it. This is true for all of us—everyone receives conditioned messages, both good and bad, from her parents, society, relationships, and experiences. Our conditioned self is how we show up in the world. It dictates everything from the way we think about money to our fear of success; how we use our great leadership skills to our display of creative prowess. It informs how much we accept ourselves for who we really are, and it can dictate how much self-love we feel we deserve (if we feel we deserve any at all).

For those of us who had less than picture-perfect childhoods (my own included narcissistic, codependent parents who struggled with alcoholism, as well as physical, verbal, and emotional abuse), this means that some of those earliest lessons are ones we won't want to carry with us throughout the rest of our lives. Instead, they're lessons that have taught us to deny, silence, and "fix" our authentic selves; to be our own harshest critics and neglect offering ourselves the time and energy we deserve to care for ourselves. Maybe they're even lessons that have cut us off from the voice of our authentic selves entirely.

The longer that we've been sharing ourselves with the world through a filter, rejecting our truest selves, and denying ourselves the care we deserve, the harder it can be to strip away that filter, embrace our authenticity, and let our truest self shine with compassion and care. Honestly, it can be downright terrifying, at times. But the good news is that every single one of us has that true self, that higher self who desperately wants to greet the world with authenticity: she's in there, even if she's been quiet for a long time.

This highest, most honest version of ourselves is most connected to our heart's desire, our soul's purpose, and the divine magic of the world. The more we work to connect with what is truly authentic to ourselves, the more we work to heal our past wounds and limiting beliefs, we become the best and most magical versions of ourselves to manifest everything that we desire.

Many of us are so uniquely talented, so passionate in what we do, so powerful in our service to others, and have so many other amazing qualities. We feel we're good people, but struggle with feelings of being "not good enough."

But think about this: every minute we badass Alpha women spend analyzing everything we don't like about ourselves is one minute of wasted energy. Add up all those minutes, and just think of what you could do: in a day, in a week, in a lifetime! Start a new business, plan your dream trip, volunteer in your community, take up a new hobby, make new friends, learn a new skill—the list is endless.

Plus, YOU DESERVE self-love and acceptance; in all your beautiful, imperfect, wild, Alpha-ness. Regardless of your success and failures, what's in your bank account or what it says on your business card—or if you even *have* a business card; in spite of your flaws and quirks (and sometimes *because* of them!) you deserve love and acceptance. You deserve self-love and acceptance simply because you are. You matter, because you are. And the world needs you, exactly as you are.

But okay, I know, I know—redirecting that energy we're so used to turning over to our inner critic is easier said than done. So here are my top three tips:

1. Identify some of your limiting beliefs, counterproductive mindsets, or habits that are holding you back. Developing that awareness is a huge step. Setting the intention to work on that awareness is an even bigger one.

2. Focus on your feelings. Ask yourself: does this belief, mindset, or habit feel good in my heart? Am I happy and thriving, or am I feeling limited, scared, worried, or negative? When you are connecting to your authentic self, you will feel good. When you are experiencing something other than authenticity, you won't feel as good.

3. Begin to connect with your own intuition. Consider trying a spiritual practice like meditation. Meditation is a great way to create a quiet, empty space where the conditioned self is not running the show—inviting your true self to come through. While you can meditate anywhere, at any time, if you're just beginning it's nice to set up a comfortable, private space for yourself. You might want to light a candle, play some soft music, or prop yourself up on your favorite pillow. Start with just five or even three minutes. Then, check in with yourself: how did it go? What did you discover? As you grow more comfortable with meditation, you might find that you enjoy extending your time to twenty or thirty minutes, or even more!

. . . .

Rewrite The Stories You Tell Yourself

....

How often do you think about the stories you tell yourself? Did you even know you tell yourself stories? (Because you do—and we ALL do—throughout the day, every day.) Anytime you begin a thought with: "Well, that's just how I am..." or "I do this because of this reason..." or "I've just always..." you're telling yourself a story about yourself. And these stories—true or false, positive or negative—inform not only your beliefs about yourself and the world around you, but the actions and behaviors that follow.

That's the power these stories can have.

Now, when the stories we tell ourselves are rooted in things like confidence, empowerment, and abundance mindset, they can be some of our greatest, secret superpowers. But more often than not, the stories we tell ourselves are out of alignment with who we truly are: rooted in insecurity, fear, unworthiness, and lack mindset. And that's why we've got to rewrite them. But rewriting the stories we tell ourselves—especially if they're stories we've been telling most of our lives—takes work.

The first step is to become aware of your stories in the first place: what do you tell yourself about yourself, and what are you actively telling others? How much real-world evidence do you actually have to back up your stories? And *hey*, do you even want them to be true in the first place? (For example telling yourself: "I am terrible with money"...real world evidence: "I maxed out my credit cards and ruined my credit, right out of college.")

Often we are subscribing to not just our own stories, but the stories of *others* as well: our parents and other influences in our lives. Stories can be generational, and any stories they created from their own past experiences—or even their own parents' stories—can influence us because we unknowingly subscribe to these beliefs in addition to our own. Some common examples are the idea that "nothing good comes easy" or "you need to struggle and suffer in order to have anything worthwhile." Once you identify that some of these stories are not even your own, it becomes easier to release them and let them go.

Once you become aware of the false or negative stories you're stuck in, it's time to think about the influence these stories have had on your life. If you rewrote some of the stories that became central to how you live your life, how would your life change? Imagine if you started telling different stories—what would that look and feel like? How might you transform, simply by shifting your narrative? For example, telling yourself: "I will start to look at my finances more closely, pay my bills on time, and be more mindful about where my money is going." This feels scary but also empowering.

Be willing to question yourself. Think about what you'd say to a good friend describing herself in a way you know is totally untrue and doesn't give nearly enough credit to the great person she truly is. The next time you feel the impulse to excuse a behavior that isn't serving you (which often sounds like "Oh, well, that's just how I am…") be willing to interrogate yourself. Is that REALLY how you "just are," or can you choose to be "just" another way? How might a different way of being serve you better? For example, if I were speaking to a friend who was being hard on herself, I would say something like "Just because you made a mistake in your early 20s doesn't mean you're doomed to keep making the same mistake for the rest of your life. Isn't it possible you learned your lesson from the past and are *less* likely to make the same mistake? It's true some people haven't made this mistake (yet) but you're in a good spot; you've already 'been there, done that' and are way wiser for it."

The same is true for the stories about experiences—you know what I'm talking about, those experiences you replay in your mind over and over again, and let it nag into a place of negativity. What if, the next time you started to relive your latest disappointing or embarrassing moment, you told yourself a different story instead? Try: "Actually, that wasn't so bad…" or "At least I learned *X, Y, Z* from that little fumble…" Suddenly, you're able to see what was once a negative story in a positive light, and your entire energy changes. (For example, when I start remembering the experience of being afraid of being evicted and feeling really scared, I can say to myself: "Even though I was afraid I would get evicted back then, I still managed to make enough money to cover the rent. In fact, I have always been able to find shelter, even when things were really bad financially.")

What about all those things you tell yourself you "should" be doing? Have you ever gotten stuck in the mindset that you "should" be living a certain life, filled with particular things, by a very specific age, with an accomplished to-do list by your side? Have you ever thought: "I should be more 'settled down' by now" or "My goals just aren't realistic for someone of my age, with my income." Again, these are all nothing more than stories. What if instead, you said to yourself: "I'm allowed to live an entire life of wild adventure" or "I deserve to work towards my dreams and live the life I desire." How might those stories change the way you live your life? Here's another example: "Everybody is more financially established than I am and I should have more savings and assets than I do now. Because I don't, I feel too discouraged and overwhelmed to even try to save." What would a different story sound like here?

Now that you've had a chance to think about some of the stories that you've been telling yourself, try to rewrite one or more of those stories into something more empowering and authentic to who you are.

Consider these examples:

> *"I learned many valuable lessons from my past money mistakes and now I am ready to use the knowledge to help my finances."*

> *"Even when things were so bad, I still managed to pay my rent and have shelter. I am actually quite resourceful with money."*

"While I may not have as much accumulated wealth as my friends do now, I am optimistic about my future and I am excited to grow my wealth rapidly."

The stories you tell yourself and the words you use have way more power than you might think. But by becoming aware of the stories you tell yourself and others, by questioning them, and by having a willingness to rewrite them, you'll be amazed at how the rest of your life—your behaviors, your beliefs, and what the universe provides—will follow. Next time you tell yourself a story, why not make it a real-life fairytale instead? (But, you know, the kind where the princess opens her own business, travels the world, or gets that PhD she's always been longing for.)

....

The Myth Of The "Hot Mess": Feeling vs. Being
....

Have you ever called yourself a "hot mess," even in jest? This is just one of the many stories we might be telling ourselves, about ourselves—and chances are, it's not serving you well. When it comes to being a "hot mess" (or any other negative self-talk you might engage in) there is a difference between *feeling* like a hot mess, and actually being one.

Let me explain: in my experience coaching women, I have met so many women who call themselves "hot messes." But what I have found through working with them is that while women might say they are a "hot mess" and even *feel* like it's true, most of them actually have more of their shit together than they realize. In fact, these women are quite talented, capable, motivated, and amazing. Rather than being completely unraveled, they're usually just experiencing struggle in one or two key aspects of their lives—things like a fear of failure, being stuck in perfectionism, unresolved past trauma, low self-confidence or feelings of unworthiness, and more. But once they work though the one really big thing holding them back they suddenly find themselves thriving, kicking ass, and feeling a whole lot better.

Here are some tips for knowing when you're just stuck in a rut, versus actually being a total and complete hot mess:

Feelings of being hot mess can arise when you are overwhelmed, unsure of yourself, and the voice of your inner critic is louder than usual. You might feel like nothing you do is good enough or meaningful enough, and you might question your self-worth or your ability to handle things.

When you're *feeling* like a hot mess, pause and...

★ *Notice three things about yourself that are pretty awesome*

★ *Acknowledge three things in your life that you are grateful for*

★ *Choose a few things (1-3) that you can say no to, quit, pause, or postpone*

★ *Take time to rest, give yourself some care, and find time to play*

However, sometimes we might ACTUALLY BE a hot mess— and it's important to acknowledge this. If you've engaged in new behaviors or taken sudden actions that are destructive to your joy and wellbeing, chances are you're going to want to consider getting serious about seeking the care and help you need. Signals that you might be deep into hot mess territory include:

★ *Compulsive use of a substance or activity to cope (alcohol, drugs, shopping, sex, exercise)*

★ *Destructive behavior that can harm yourself or those around you (physically or emotionally)*

★ *Impulsive behaviors that are a detriment to your job, business, finances, or relationships*

★ *Anything that directly prevents you from thriving*

And hey, if it turns out you *do* identify as a hot mess, now is a great time to own up and seek help: from working with a therapist who offers different behavioral counseling options or medications to working with healers and life coaches who have experience with clients suffering from issues similar to yours. There are plenty of options for help and self-care that will allow you to feel safe and understood, while working through whatever challenges you're currently facing. And don't forget to reach out to loved ones as well! So many of us have been a bit (or more than a bit) of a "hot mess" at different points in our lives, and we get you, Sister. Start with the professionals, but don't forget about that sisterhood you have waiting with open arms behind you.

. . . .

Cut The Cord: An Energetic Practice

....

Cord cutting is an intentional energetic practice designed to preserve and protect you from all external energies, people, and experiences that have the potential to catch your attention, latch onto you, and drain you of your energy. Think of your "cords" as figurative attachments to anything that is imbalanced in your life—any relationship or situation in which you're giving far more than you're receiving, and that is starting to become a burden to you. Often times we form these cords with people in our lives (past and present) and they are often loved ones. When we tend to be people-pleasing or codependent, have a lack of boundaries, or hang on to strong attachments, we form energetic cords with others. Sometimes you can form an energetic cord with a thing as well, like a house or job, and your attachment to these objects starts affecting your energy. In this situation, a cord-cutting practice can be helpful in creating energetic detachment and freedom.

Through this meditation practice, you'll lovingly sever these cords, release yourself from any burdensome attachments, and free your energy to be utilized in more balanced and productive ways.

But note: cord cutting is just designed to relieve you of any "energetic" cords that aren't serving you. This doesn't mean that you're ending a relationship, leaving a job, removing yourself from a particular experience, or ceasing to love and care for who or what you're cord cutting from. In fact, with this practice, you can still maintain these relationships, and love whatever or whoever you're "cutting cords" from. They can even still be a big part of your life!

In this instance, you're simply cutting the energetic connection between yourself and this person or situation, taking back control of your own energy. By doing this, the other person's energy, emotional state, intention or action, suffering, thoughts, and manifestations no longer play tug-of-war with your own energy. This is the healthy, natural way of living—each of us needs to be in full control of our own energies. And, let's get real here: there are some people who can be described as "energy vampires" —and yeah, they can be super annoying and exhausting. The best way to prevent them from sucking your energy out of you is by getting really intentional about taking back your energy and protecting it. Cord cutting is a great way to start. That way, you're protected from "energy vampires" and they become self-reliant (or, just find another victim. As long as it's not YOU!).

In my own life, I have used cord cutting meditations for specific people and relationships. My parents, for example, were informative to my past experiences and traumas as well as my conditioned beliefs and fears, so a cord-cutting meditation was helpful. I've also used it in my business as well, when others are drawn to my energy in ways that become unhealthy, and thereby draining and depressing to my own energy (with difficult past clients or a draining project, for example).

If this sounds a little too woo for you, try to be open-minded and see if you start to notice a shift in how you feel—especially if you have been struggling with things that drain your energy and overwhelm you. It can be very healing and empowering to move forward with your authentic, grounded self—free of the energetic burdens of others.

Cord Cutting Visualization

Now, take a moment to settle yourself and close your eyes.

Imagine your energy as a calming, clear light, surrounding your being— inhaling as you inhale, exhaling as you exhale, moving as you move, becoming still as you become still. With each inhale, draw this cleansing light into you and closer around you. Pull this bright, light energy into your being.

Imagine a figure 8 or infinity symbol written in the ground, surrounded by beautiful white light that is sacred and protected. Imagine yourself inside one circle, and the person/thing you are cutting cords from inside the other circle.

Begin to imagine drawing the light into the areas of your body and mind where you might be holding tightness, tension, physical stress, or emotional burdens. These are the areas where you may have formed the cords or attachments. Notice if you can see or visualize these cords. Notice where in your body these cords are, and where on the other person's body they are attached.

As you continue to breathe, imagine sharp, bright rays of light severing the energetic cords between you and your burdens. As the cords are severed, notice their ends fray, then break up, dissolve, and release. You are free.

Let the light swirl through these areas, cleansing and healing, filling you with a sense of release and freedom. Let yourself receive this energy without a sense of guilt or obligation. Send loving, healing energy to the other person and offer love and gratitude to your higher self for facilitating this practice. Then, when you are ready, finish the practice by opening your eyes.

. . . .

Set Boundaries (And Stick To Them)

....

Boundaries are probably the most significant way you can preserve the hard work of healing you've done—so setting boundaries and sticking to them is pretty important. Many people think setting boundaries is all about (and *only* about) saying no—to requests, to jobs, to social events, to how much you show up for others, etc. But having clear and strong boundaries is so much more than just saying no; in fact, consider it more so as saying yes to YOURSELF and putting your needs and energy first.

There are many different types of boundaries an Alpha Sister needs in order to stay whole and energetically healthy: emotional boundaries, energetic boundaries, boundaries of resources like time and money, boundaries concerning the behaviors we're willing to tolerate in others. All of these boundaries are critical when it comes to taking care of ourselves and protecting our energy.

Emotional and energetic boundaries are some of the most important boundaries you can set—they're designed to protect you when people or situations are draining you of your energy, making demanding requests of your time and resources, or relying on you beyond what you're able or willing to give. In these situations, without clear boundaries, you'll inevitably end up absorbing negative external energy or giving too much of your positive energy. Either way, you'll become depleted—and that's the last thing you want or need.

Professional boundaries are also hugely important—whether you own a business or work for someone else. If you tend to be a nurturer or find yourself taking ownership or responsibility of your team or co-workers' success, these are clear signs that a boundary needs to be set. Boundaries around work/life balance are key as well, in order to ensure that you're not giving so much of yourself to your job that you have nothing left for the rest of your life.

But setting boundaries can be difficult—especially for Alpha Women who feel like we can "handle it all." But just because you are capable of handling something doesn't mean you should allow people with draining energy and destructive behaviors into your life to feed off of your high vibes and deplete you of resources. Just because you have the capacity to take on more doesn't mean you're obligated to do so—so don't jeopardize or threaten your boundaries just because you think you can take on more. You don't owe anyone or anything your energy. Once you set your boundaries, guard them fiercely. Treat yourself with the same love and care you'd treat your friends and family.

Get clear on what some of your boundaries might be—especially what behaviors, energies, or emotions are non-negotiable to you. Don't compromise on your boundaries. What things set off warning bells in your mind? What sorts of vibes trigger you? Be aware of the things you can't tolerate. Consider taking the space below to list a few; this way, if you find yourself struggling with or questioning your boundaries, you'll be able to return to this list and remind yourself of your priorities and what needs your protecting.

My Boundaries and Non-negotiables:

_____

_____

_____

_____

_____

_____

_____

_____

_____

_____

_____

_____

Okay, but let's say you've lapsed in one area or another—you let someone or something in that totally drained you, and now your energy is depressed and low. There are plenty of practices you can do to cleanse and replenish your energy once it has been drained. Some of my favorites include spending time with nature, savoring a nutrient-packed meal, meditating, journaling, getting a massage, or other healing practices like reiki and burning incense. Anything that fills you up with high vibes is a totally valid energy replenishing practice. Use the space below to list your favorite energetic self-care practices—this way, you'll know exactly what to do if a time comes when you need to refresh and reset.

My Favorite Energetic Self-Care Practices:

_____

_____

_____

_____

_____

_____

_____

_____

_____

Remember: you're entitled to your boundaries and it's up to you to protect them. Setting boundaries doesn't make you a less giving, uncompassionate, or disengaged person. Boundaries are your way of preserving your energy so you can show up in the world in a way that will be of best service to yourself and those around you. When someone or something comes your way, ready to drain you of your much-needed energy, send that person or thing some light and love, and wish them well—but keep your doors closed.

....

Forgiveness Is The Magic F-Word

. . . .

When it comes to f-words, forgiveness is definitely NOT my favorite one. (If you know me personally, you know what word is.) Honestly, no other f-word used to make me shut down faster or feel completely knotted up inside more than forgiveness. And that's because I didn't feel ready to forgive.

Earlier in my life, I didn't want to forgive. I felt like "they"—the people in my life, the people not in my life, past experiences, poor behaviors—didn't deserve forgiveness. Instead, I felt that cutting them (the people, the experiences, the behaviors) completely *out* of my current life was an easier, cleaner way to deal with it all, and that doing so would get me the results I desired. (Spoiler alert: I was wrong.)

When I started my personal development journey years ago, my coach at the time recognized this—at first tiptoeing around the idea of forgiveness, and then eventually pushing me headfirst into the reality that I would not achieve the results I was looking for without addressing the "huge monster in the room": my refusal to forgive past traumas.

Not surprisingly, this made me feel pretty vulnerable—calling out the brokenness I hadn't been ready to deal with. But the Alpha Female in me (brave, committed to my work) decided to sit with the discomfort, the knots in my stomach, the tears and rage, the sadness and defensiveness, and so much more, and work through that shit. Once and for all.

What followed were weeks and weeks of self-exploration and work around my "forgiveness issue." I realized that my complete rejection of forgiveness came from a fear of "becoming undone." Basically, my internal narrative went something like this:

"If I forgive them, that means they are free to enter my life again."

"If they enter my life again, they are free to bring all the old drama, pain, and destruction to my life."

"If that happens, all the work I've done on myself will get totally fucked up." (Ah, there's my favorite f-word.)

"I can't let that happen."

That was some heavy shit to carry—and if you've been there, you know what I mean. But once I explored *why* I was afraid of forgiveness, I was able to start working through it. For me, it was essential to work through my issues with someone else: a coach, a mentor, a healer, or a therapist—someone who will call you out, hold you accountable to doing the hard work, and help you see the truths and the untruths of the stories you've been telling yourself.

If this sounds familiar—and if you think you're ready to do the work of forgiveness, consider trying some of the exercises that worked for me.

★ Redefining what "forgiveness" means and in my case, my former definition of forgiveness meant those people and things I were forgiving got to start over with a blank slate. But for most people, that's not going to happen. Instead, I developed a new definition for forgiveness—one of freedom from the terrible feelings and fears I had been living with for years.

★ Setting boundaries which required learning more about how and why to set boundaries in the first place—and this needed to happen in my personal life, my business, and my relationships. The result of setting more effective boundaries was that I would no longer feel powerless and helpless about deciding to reconnect with those I was trying to forgive. I realized that I was in complete control of allowing others access to or influence in my life... and that, Alpha Sisters, was EMPOWERING.

★ Healing the inner child because chances are, if you're dealing with forgiveness, your issues stem from way-back-when. In my case, working to heal my inner child and teenager released me from the paralyzing fear and anger left over from pain experienced by my younger self.

★ Tapping into the logical mind by using my adult, logical mind, I was able to reevaluate my past with less of the emotions that went with it. For example, I was finally able to see the mother of my past as someone who was, back then, younger than I am now—someone struggling with terrible self-esteem and insecurity, stuck in an unhappy marriage, and trying to navigate her life as though there was nothing wrong. By doing that work, I was able to find compassion and patience towards that young woman who was just doing the best she could with what she had.

In my own experience, it took a while to get to a place of forgiveness of my past—but I have. And I have to admit that forgiveness *really* is a magic f-word. (Just maybe not the only one.) When you're finally able to free yourself from all the pain, emotions, fears, and resistance that are connected to forgiving your past, it's incredible how much space is created—space that will allow you to invite something new into your life, something that is more fun, joyful, and loving for your soul.

. . . .

Ho'oponopono: A Forgiveness Practice

....

While each and every culture around the world has their own
systems of justice and reconciliation and practices for forgiveness,
the practice we'll explore here is one that originates in ancient
Hawaii—but can be practiced anywhere, at any time, whenever
you might need to call upon it.

The Ho'oponopono Practice

Ho'oponopono is an ancient Hawaiian practice of forgiveness
and reconciliation. When people practice the same prayer over
the course of hundreds of years—a prayer like Ho'oponopono—
it can generate a magnificent energetic resonance and healing
power, which can be harnessed to help anyone interested in
practicing it today. In today's language, Ho'oponopono might
sound something like this:

"I am sorry."
"Please forgive me."
"Thank you."
"I love you."

These aren't complicated phrases, but don't be surprised if you notice yourself responding with thoughts like: "I am *not* sorry"; "I have done nothing wrong"; "I am not the one to forgive." If you find yourself becoming fired up, I hear you—maybe what you need to ask forgiveness for, or what you need to forgive, were through no fault of your own. It is important to understand that the Ho'oponopono practice isn't about placing blame or responsibility for any hurt or wrongdoing. It is simply a loving prayer designed to help you release your burdens and be free. So even if you're hesitant, I encourage you to try this practice anyway. If you find it impossible to practice Ho'oponopono that probably means you have a really strong hold on your trauma and you may not be ready to let go. In this case, you may need to seek some additional help, personal or professional, to work through this resistance.

How to Perform Ho'oponopono Practice

Ready to practice Ho'oponopono for yourself? First, here's how to pronounce it: in the Hawaiian language each vowel is pronounced as its own, separate syllable. So "Ho'oponopono", which also includes an accent mark, is pronounced: 'ho-oh-po-no-po-no." This is crucial for understanding the nuances of the Hawaiian language, in order to perform Ho'oponopono with respect and mindfulness.

Begin by sitting in a quiet place. Light a candle, have a cup of tea, play relaxing music—do whatever will best invite you into a state of peace and reflection. Take a few deep breaths. Start to visualize the person(s), entity (or entities), or thing(s) you would like to forgive and release. Note: if thinking of the specific subject of harm is triggering to you, you can skip this step and, instead, set an intention for forgiving *everything* that you need to release, in order to live at your highest vibration. Finally, slowly start repeating "ho-oh-po-no-po-no" while trying to embody the energy of the four messages the phrase represents:

"I am sorry."
"Please forgive me."
"Thank you."
"I love you."

As you sit with this practice, imagine yourself being showered with a beautiful pink light of love from head to toe, a light that envelops you, shields you from negative energy, and invites you into a state of forgiveness, acceptance, and release.

. . . .

'ho-oh-po-no-po-no'

Nurture Your Mental And Physical Wellness

....

When it comes to nurturing ourselves, whether emotionally, physically, or energetically, I think many of us struggle with finding the space to do it. When I say "space," what I mean is time, permission, resources, willingness, opportunities... all of it.

We may say "I need to manage my stress better," but in reality we might never allow ourselves the space to realize what that actually means to us; what our individual, authentic souls need in order to manage our stress, what's actually causing our stress, and how to minimize that stress in our lives in the first place. Often, we take a Band-Aid approach to stress. (Think: "I got that one-hour massage squeezed into my busy day; now I can cross 'manage my stress better' off my to-do list." You know what I mean?) It's not really helpful to keep adding things onto an already-full plate, without creating the space for those things first.

When our lives are too jam-packed with things (to-do lists, work and career, emotions, people, worries, intentions and goals, and more) we don't fully have the space to nurture our own healing and wellness.

But how do we create that space in the first place? As high-performing Alpha Women, we don't even know where to start sometimes, right? It's easy for us to become paralyzed by space: how to create it in the first place, and then how to nurture the space we just created without filling it up with more tasks and objectives.

It's something I've had to do in my own life, and lucky you, you get to learn from my hard-won lessons here. Check out these tips on how I got better at creating intentional space in order to take care of myself in more fulfilling ways.

★ Asking myself: "Is this fun?" At some point, I realized I had no idea how to just let go and have fun for the sake of FUN. Sure, my daily life felt fun: I enjoyed my work, I enjoyed leading retreats, I enjoyed connecting with the sisterhood of Alphas I had built. I was pretty sure I knew how to have fun. But it turned out, I actually had no idea how to create and enjoy frivolous, indulgent fun without a higher purpose to something or someone. The kind of fun I truly needed was the kind we had as kids, when there was no timeline, no agenda, and no obligation. In order to create some space in my life, I had to be very intentional about exploring and defining what fun meant to me when I created it for no other reason than to enjoy.

★ Releasing guilt. I also discovered that guilt was creating a huge energy block in my life, preventing me from reaching the mental and physical wellness I desired. I struggled with guilt for not working even harder than I already was, guilt for not serving more people, guilt for not giving more—feeling selfish every time I took care of myself, guilt over past actions, even guilt over my thoughts and feelings. The thing is, guilt is a totally useless energy—one that doesn't benefit ourselves or anyone else. All it does is bum us out, hold us back, and prevent us from growing. Guilt also takes up a lot of space. The sooner I was able to release the guilt I was holding on to, the sooner I was able to transform my life and take actions to help myself and others in more positive ways.

★ Investing in self-pleasure. Self-care can look like a lot of different things and it's important to find what works for you. For me, allowing myself lavish luxuries like massages and spa treatments works well. For many people, it can be a struggle to believe that spending time and hard-earned money on things that might seem "useless" or "frivolous," purely for one's own pleasure, is worthwhile. At first, it took effort for me to care for myself, especially when I felt I "shouldn't" invest in that beauty treatment or get a massage mid-weekday. But once I started caring for myself, I realized my beliefs about investing in self-care (that I would go broke, that my business would suffer, that people would judge me, that my world might fall apart) were all rooted in my own self-judgment and fear. News flash: when you take care of yourself, NOTHING BAD HAPPENS. In fact, a lot of good things happen. Learning to seek my own pleasure allowed me to develop self-deserving and self-love mindsets, which actually ended up attracting *more* abundance to my life. Well worth it, in my opinion.

....

The Big O – Yep, We're Going There

....

Yes, ladies. I'm talking about orgasms: a major pathway to embodying feminine energy. Because believe it or not, one of the best ways to tap into your powerful, feminine energy is through experiencing an orgasm.

Our female organs—their functions, abilities, strengths, adaptabilities, sensations, and powers—are one thing that really sets women apart from men. The womb comes with its own innate wisdom. It's the wisdom to *create* at all levels, including one of the deepest and most profound levels of creation: that of creating another human being, with a soul. Plus, the energy center of the womb, the sacral chakra, is the hub of your emotions, sensuality, and the creative, generative energy you bring to everything you do. It can also influence your flow and vibration. Basically, the womb is where your body holds space for all kinds of wild, beautiful magic. So what better way to really feel the divine feminine power within you than through the "Big O"?

During my years of coaching many Alpha Sisters, of all different ages and backgrounds—each one a powerful leader, talented creator, and all-around badass—quite a surprising number had never experienced an orgasm. WTF? This, ladies, is not okay. It is time to claim orgasm as one of your regular Alpha Woman practices.

By the way, it's really not hard to take care of this. And you definitely don't need a partner in order to do so. Master orgasm as a self-practice whether you have a partner or not. (This is what electronics and online shopping were made for! Women today are surrounded by great resources and tools.) No ifs, ands, or buts about it. If you consider yourself an empowered woman who wants to embrace her feminine energy and all its magic, get friendly with your feminine power source, stat.

. . . .

Everything You Ever Wanted To Know About Breast Massage

....

We just talked about pleasuring yourself to get connected with the "Big O" (aka orgasm). Now, are you up for taking one step toward really embracing your feminine energy in a sexy, self-care promoting way? Ladies: we're about to dive into breast massage.

Breast massage is a method of giving loving care to some other lady parts—and believe it or not, it's been practiced as a celebration of femininity and self-care for *thousands* of years. Plus, breast massage has great health benefits, from enhancing the function of your lymphatic system, to increasing blood flow, to relieving stress. (And because the biological composition of the breasts can make them a site for environmental toxin buildup, it's especially important to take care of your girls.)

Breast massage has magical benefits, too: it can open and heal your heart chakra—the space where you connect to your higher, divine female self, and where you can seek and receive answers to your questions of healing. It increases the circulation of energy through the body (and can even release anti-aging hormones like prolactin, oxytocin, and estrogen!), and is also where love and healing for yourself and others come from. Talk about magic.

Regular breast massage can help you get more comfortable with the idea of pleasuring yourself and giving loving touches to your own body—especially if you're always giving that care and affection to other people. Plus, the connection to your own magic and creative power is through pleasure: what feels good in your body. Breast massage is a great way to start working through any shame, embarrassment, or guilt you might have around pleasuring yourself, healing any traumas or blocks you might have. It's crucial to you unlocking your power. (And it's fun!)

....

BREAST MASSAGE
+ LYMPHATIC HEALTH FOR YOUR "GIRLS"
+ OPENS HEART CHAKRA + SELF-LOVE THRU PLEASURE

SELF-MASSAGE HOW-TO

Massage from center of heart chakra from inside out in circular motion.

THEN REVERSE DIRECTION

With one hand over & one hand under breast, massage in half circle motion in each direction. Do this with each breast.

Massage each breast from the nipple to outside in circular motion.

Feel free to continue with whatever feels nurturing and pleasurable for you.

Breast Massage Oil Recipe

....

Mix these with 2 fl oz of carrier oil (coconut or jojoba). Store in a small glass container.

8 drops Rose – for love, feminine power, and strengthening/balancing the heart chakra

8 drops Geranium – for hormonal and emotional balance, inner peace, and happiness

6 drops Orange – for energy purifying and healing

5 drops Ylang Ylang – promotes estrogen health, sensuality, relaxation, and fights depression

For added magic, drop a small tumbled stone of rose quartz into the mixture for 24 hours, or let the oil sit under the full moon for a night.

BREAST OIL

8 DROPS ROSE   8 DROPS GERANIUM

6 DROPS ORANGE   5 DROPS YLANG YLANG

Journaling, Your Way

. . . .

Journaling is a great practice for Alpha Sister growth—whether you are generating new ideas for your education, business, and career; working out some hard-to-handle feelings with a pen and paper; or just eager to figure out the ending to that recurring dream you can never quite remember, the benefits of keeping a journal (or, you know, several) are practically endless. (Plus, it's fun!) Sure, not every Alpha Sister is going to be a natural journal-keeper. But if you're looking to get your creative juices flowing, mix up your mindfulness practice, or just feel like trying something new, this chapter offers some basic tips for getting started—and loving it.

★ **Gratitude Journaling**

A favorite of the Alpha Female Sisterhood, gratitude journals are a beautiful practice for both brightening your day (who doesn't feel better after thinking about all the great stuff they've got going on?) and increasing the abundance in your life. The more you recognize all the good stuff the universe has sent your way, the more the universe wants to send. Aim to journal about five or ten things you're grateful for every day (and WHY—the why is key) and feel the abundance flow. Journaling about why you feel thankful is an awesome way to up your gratitude vibe.

★ **Bullet Journaling**

Love lists? In that case, a bullet journal is definitely worth a try. Whether you're using this journal to organize your day, your life, your business, your goals, or your wildest dreams, bullet journaling is a great way to get all the thoughts dancing around your mind out of your head and onto the page with clarity. There are also lots of cool stickers and other accessories for bullet journaling—and honestly, how fun is that?

★ **Vision Journaling**

If you're an Alpha boss, you're probably familiar with a vision board. But have you considered a vision journal? Break out those colored pencils and doodle the most magical vision of your best life, brainstorm the business of your dreams, or just plot a fun project you've been eager to get rolling on. Let your mind—and your pen—run wild! This creative, more laid-back form of journaling can help you unlock the sacral chakra (your creative energy center) and help you become more effective in visualizing and manifesting.

★ **Dream Journaling**

Ever have a vivid, meaningful dream—one that you absolutely cannot remember when you wake up, no matter how hard you try? Stop losing those messages from your unconscious brain and signals from the universe by keeping a dream journal bedside. Not only will a dream journal help you remember your dreams come morning, it'll also give you space to analyze them and learn more about how that beautiful brain of yours really works. Be sure to keep this journal on your nightstand and create a habit of jotting down your dream as soon as you wake up. As you start keeping your dream journal, your dreams may get a bit wilder and more vivid—this is validation that your expansion through dreaming is happening, so stick with the practice.

★ **Writing Letters**

When it comes to putting your thoughts, feelings, ideas, and dreams down on paper sometimes journaling just isn't going to cut it: you need someone to write to. Letter writing—whether you end up sending those words off with a stamp or not—is a great way to connect with yourself and what you're really feeling. Consider writing a letter to your younger self, your future self, someone you love, a person you might have a tense relationship with, a public figure, your community, or even the universe.

★ **Affirmation Journaling**

Affirmations are a great way to change your thoughts, self-talk, and energy—and we could all use more positive words in our daily lives, right? An affirmations journal, whether you're writing your own affirmations or saving and savoring the words of others, is the perfect place to be gentle, encouraging, and supportive of yourself—and to remind yourself what a badass babe you are. The key to affirmation journaling is trying to FEEL the affirmations while you are journaling. So, instead of repetitively recording affirmations, try to access the energy and emotions of those powerful affirmations as well.

★ **Timed Journaling**

If you struggle with setting your authentic self free, or if you're always editing yourself, timed journaling might be an exercise for you. Set an egg timer (or your cell phone—but no interruptions allowed!) for five minutes, and then let the words fly. Don't stop writing until the timer goes off, even if you're not sure you have much to say. You might be surprised by what comes out. And hey, you might even learn something new about yourself or discover clarity in a current struggle. Try not to read or edit while you are writing.

★ **Free Writing (also called Automatic Writing)**

Similar to timed journaling, free writing is an exercise designed to help you tap into your subconscious self. With free writing, once you press that pen to the page you're not to pick it up again until all your thoughts are out of your head and onto the paper. Whether it's just a few minutes or an hour (you'll be surprised how time flies when you're in a flow) any amount of free writing is great for generating new ideas, releasing suppressed burdens, uncovering hidden feelings, connecting to your higher self, jump-starting creativity, or looking at yourself in a new way.

. . . .

"Life is short. Don't miss it. Don't let others dictate your journey, your healing, your grief, your projects, your focus or YOU. Be here now...wherever here is for you."
−Michelle M.

Your Journaling Space

. . . .

Know Your Awesomeness: 100 Ways To Awesome

. . . .

This is one of my favorite self-love practices—and it's one that I always recommend to my clients and the members of the Alpha Female Sisterhood—so consider it a must-do! It's called 100 Ways of Awesomeness, and it's a great practice for snapping out of that "not good enough" mentality you might be harboring and instead embracing your gifts, celebrating your power, and totally owning how awesome you really are. Any time you find yourself playing small, not going after your dreams, not living in line with your purpose, or not doing the things you truly want to do, this exercise is a great way to shake you out of your limiting mindset and shift your energy into one of "I can do this and I WILL do this."

But first, a tip: many people who start this practice don't wind up finishing it. Believe me when I say that its power lies in truly seeing it through from beginning to end. The good news is all you need is a notebook, a writing utensil, and a little bit of time on your hands.

100 Ways of Awesomeness

Start by grabbing a piece of paper and marking it with the numbers 1–100. Then, begin writing down all the ways that you're awesome. It's that simple! But, in case you get stuck, I've included some tips as well.

Tip 1: As you start writing, you might notice the exercise flows easily. The first several ways you're awesome will probably come to you pretty quickly. But then, it's going to get harder as you go on. Depending on your self-confidence level, your self-worth, and your self-acceptance, you're probably going to get stuck. The key is, when you do get stuck, don't quit. Stay with the discomfort, reach within yourself, and keep writing.

Tip 2: Don't judge your list. You don't have to show anyone your list, either. This exercise is not about what a great list you put together as much as it's about sitting in the vibration of your awesomeness, both during and after the exercise. Even when you get stuck, reach inward to figure out why you're still awesome. Don't get caught up in the quality of your list, but rather focus on the energetic shift generated by the exercise itself.

Tip 3: Do not get help writing your list. Do not ask your friends, do not ask your partner, do not ask your kids, do not ask your co-workers. This is a self-development exercise, so the entire purpose is to get you to empower yourself to shift your energy. YOURSELF. It's all about you and your self-empowerment. It might be tempting, but do not get help.

Tip 4: If you do stop this exercise mid-list and don't complete it in one sitting, when you are ready to complete your list again you must start from the beginning. Just like a marathon, you cannot run in sprints and bursts whenever you feel like it. In order to achieve the full energetic benefits of this exercise you need to complete the list, 1-100, all in one sitting. (And no cheating by copying your old list! Do the exercise from scratch.)

Tip 5: Revisit this exercise periodically whenever you feel like you need it. You'll start to notice that the more you do this exercise, the more you'll be able to embrace your power, celebrate your gifts, recognize your magic, acknowledge what a great person you are, and enjoy all the positive things about yourself. You'll also notice that the more you recognize your own awesomeness, the more others will recognize it too. Then, the universe will begin to support you and your efforts even more—only good things will come of it, guaranteed.

Now, after you do this exercise, what do you do next? Ask yourself: what are you going to do with this amazing awesomeness and high-vibration energy that you just generated? Hopefully, you use it to make a difference: in your work, in your life, in your family, in your community, in the world.

....

Part 4
A Sprinkle of Magic

Your Intuition, Your Soul, And Your Higher Self

....

If you look up the origin of the word "intuition" it is a combination of the prefix "in" (aka "inside") and "tuition" (which can signify protection, knowledge, and guidance). Looking at this, we can see why so many people consider intuition to be their personal, inner GPS system.

This is what I believe to be true, garnered from all the readings, studying, and magical communications I've experienced with my spirit guides, higher self, and other spirits I've connected with as a shaman: we are all souls having a human experience. Each soul has experienced multiple lifetimes before this exact human experience as ourselves, and after we die our souls will continue on.

Every soul also has certain lessons and purposes they need to fulfill during each human lifetime. As they reincarnate as humans (essentially, becoming you and me for a lifetime) these souls might have some memory of their past lives and lessons, but we—the people these souls become—don't have any memories or knowledge of what came before. Sometimes we might get hints or vague memories of our past lives (for example, a certain familiarity with a particular culture or language, a dream or vivid image of certain lifestyle, experience, or environment that we can't quite explain). Nothing from our current life would suggest we'd know these things or have these images stored in our memories, but they're there—and there are a lot of resources about researching past lives if that's something you're curious to learn more about.

You may have heard the term "higher self." Higher self is the part of our own soul that's the most authentic, magical, and divine. Our higher self is all-knowing, especially about our life purpose and soul experiences, and stays in the divine realm to guide us. So, when we mention that we are connecting with our own intuition, we are being guided and protected by the divine, source, and/or god, and also our higher self: that part of our own soul that's most connected to the divine. The more open and connected we are to our higher self, the more authentic, magical, and joyful version of ourselves we become. Meditation and spiritual work is really about improving our communication and clarity—and deepening our trust and faith—with this connection.

. . . .

Protect Your Energy

....

Another topic that frequently comes up between myself and my clients is the practice of protecting your energy. This is a really important self-care practice, especially for anyone who is particularly energy sensitive—also known as empaths or clairsentient people. For these people—or anyone who is sharply tuned into the energy around them—energy protection is a key to being able to navigate the world without becoming overwhelmed or absorbing any energy that you don't want taking up space in your body, heart, and mind.

Sometimes we may need to protect our energy because of a negative or challenging situation we are dealing with, like an emotional crisis, a difficult relationship, or even "haters"/"frenemies" throwing you energetic shade. So learning how to protect your own energy is an effective and powerful skill.

There is a myth that in order to protect your energy, you need external tools like sage for smudging or healing crystals. While these can help, it's important you know that you already have the most effective and powerful tool for protecting your energy within you: yourself. The most important thing to recognize is that you are fully in charge of your own energy. You should feel empowered to know you can manage and maintain the vibes that you're absorbing and putting back out into the world. Instead of feeling passive, stressed, or afraid to show up for fear of draining your energy, know that your energy is YOURS: you own it. You are in charge of raising it, managing it, maintaining it, and protecting it when necessary.

Here are tips on protecting your own energy:

★ Maintain your own high-vibration state of being by nurturing the most authentic and joyful version of yourself and putting positive energy out into the world around you. By law of attraction, your positive vibe state will only attract energies of similar vibration, naturally repelling any negative or low vibe energy.

★ Be mindful of grounding yourself—through meditation, yoga, time spent in nature—and using the earth's natural energy to recharge and protect your own.

★ Use specific visualizations—it's like you "putting on your armor," so to speak. Imagine yourself surrounded by an impenetrable bubble of positive energy, or "zipping yourself up" to keep the negative vibes out.

★ Utilize the power of crystals and other high-vibration items. Some of the crystals known for best protecting you from negative energy are black onyx, black tourmaline, hematite, jet, and smoky quartz.

. . . .

Everyone's A Little Bit Psychic

....

What is the first image that comes to mind when you think of a psychic? Someone sitting in a booth at a fairground, draped in sequined scarves and holding a crystal ball? An incense-filled basement with an old woman spreading tarot cards around a felt-covered folding table? Every movie M. Night Shyamalan has ever made?

Well buckle up, Sisters, because we're about to get real woo, real fast.

What would you think if I told you that everyone's a little bit psychic? Yep, even YOU.

In contemporary Western culture, being psychic has plenty of weird (and inaccurate) stereotypes. But personally, I think all human beings are at least a little bit psychic—and I think you'd be surprised how many people are *more* than a little bit psychic and are just keeping it to themselves. Let me break it down to you.

If you believe all human beings have souls (and I do) then think of "being psychic" as nothing more than the connection between our soul and the universe. Or our soul and God. Or the source, or the universal intelligence—whatever higher power you identify with. "Being psychic" is just being tapped into your intuitive gifts.

Basically, if you believe you have a soul and you believe that soul came from *somewhere*, then you might want to consider believing that your soul is still a little bit connected to that divine source, driving your intuition, and offering you—if you're up for calling it that—a psychic gift. Hence we're all a little bit psychic.

Sound a little too woo-woo for you?

Consider this: when was the last time you experienced *déjà vu*? Have you ever had the experience of thinking about someone and then there they are, standing right across the street? How often do you pick up your phone to call someone, only to discover that they texted you only minutes ago? Have you ever dreamed of something and then it actually happened? Do you follow the "vibes" you receive from people—forming (or *not* forming) relationships with them based on the energy you picked up in their presence?

Everyone has experienced at least some of these things, to some degree or another. And that, Alphas, is what being a little bit psychic is.

Now, some of us—especially those of us who specifically identify as psychic, intuitive, or empaths—have stronger or more intuitive connections than others. And because we have those stronger connections, the vibes, feelings, messages, ideas, sounds, and images can appear stronger as well, allowing us to channel that energy and use our gifts to help not only ourselves, but others. Some of us are clairvoyant—able to see things; some of us are clairaudient—able to hear things; some of us are claircognizant—able to just know things; and some of us are clairsentient—able to feel things. Many people have a combination of these gifts. And just because you don't claim the gift, at least publicly, doesn't mean you don't have it.

One caveat: what do I mean when I say *see things, hear things, know things*? Basically, intuitive visions, sounds, and awareness are all energetic. It's the ability to tune into your vibration and the energy you're carrying and to discern what things are aligned with that vibration. In other words: what might be a *possibility* for you, in your life, if you continue forward with the vibration and energy you're carrying. It's up to you, through your own free will, intention, and action, to actually make that intuitive "vision" occur (or, if it's not so good, avoid it completely.)

So now that I've piqued your interest, you might be wondering: if we're all a little bit psychic, how can I nurture my psychic gifts?

Everybody has the ability to work on tuning into their intuitive gifts and developing a stronger connection. In my experience, meditation and manifesting are two of the best ways to cultivate your innate psychic abilities. Think of it like nothing more than starting a conversation with the universe. And call it whatever you want, but embracing your psychic or intuitive gifts is the key to really embracing your innate power and manifesting what you desire.

....

A Meditation For Alpha Sisters

....

I know, I know—if there's one thing us badass bosses aren't good at, it's probably sitting still. Quietly. Thinking slow thoughts to ourselves. But if the idea of meditating has you running in the opposite direction (or, in this case, flipping to the end of this book) listen up: with benefits of everything from reduced stress and anxiety, to increased focus and memory, to mega self-awareness and relaxation, meditating is one of the best practices an Alpha Sister can initiate for herself.

While meditating can be seriously intimidating, frustrating, painful, (insert whatever negative descriptor you identify with here), it doesn't have to be! You can start with as little as three minutes. Just get yourself to a quiet place (or close your office door, sit in your parked car, etc.) and settle into a comfortable seat. Bonus points if you actually take the time to recline on the floor—but if you're new at this, (or, you know, if your office floor hasn't been swept in a while) no pressure! The point is to settle your body as comfortably as possible.

As you begin, keep these three reminders nearby:

1. Don't make meditating hard! In the way that true, high-performing Alpha Sisters tend to be, it might be easy to succumb to the belief that the more structured, rigid, and challenging we make our meditation practice, the better results we will get. But this is total bullshit. The mindset that if we work harder at meditating, or make it more visibly challenging (aka demonstrate to others that we are going through the effort and hardship of sticking with it) we will be somehow rewarded with faster and better results is nonsense. So resist the temptation to make it hard on yourself. Focus on making it an easy, simple, no-brainer practice.

2. Don't expect magic (at least, not the first time.) Many of us have read about or heard from people who experience so much clarity, divine guidance, healing, or other magical moments while meditating; and because of that, we tend to expect "something to happen" when we meditate. When it doesn't, we can get disappointed and frustrated, or wonder if we're "meditating wrong." What you need to realize is that even for those people who really do experience magic during meditation, their typical, day-to-day meditation practice isn't all that remarkable. Those moments of clarity and divine awareness are rare, unexpected, and often fleeting. And they tend to come more readily when we show up expecting nothing.

3. Don't substitute another activity for meditation. If you find yourself thinking thoughts like: "running is my meditation" or "drawing is my meditation" or "journaling is my form of meditation," take a pause and think again. This is something we hear a lot—and it happens when people are trying to convince

themselves that other, more enjoyable activities are a substitute ("their form") of meditation. But just because an activity you love provides a peace of mind and clarity similar to meditation, it's not actually meditating. Keep doing those awesome activities that provide you enjoyment and clarity, but also invest your time and energy in a few minutes of regular meditation. There's a definite difference and you'll notice it.

There are so many resources to help you start your meditation practice: plenty of apps you can download, or guided meditation videos and audio recordings you can find online. Your local yoga studio probably even offers a class or two on meditation. Tap into all of these available resources as you get started, but eventually build your own practice to a place where you feel comfortable meditating without another person's guidance. Nurture your practice to the point where you can have a quiet space between you, your higher self, and the divine universe.

Until then, here is one meditation I created for you. Try reading the following words to yourself, silently or quietly aloud:

I am here, open, and ready. I sit in the presence of love, gratitude, kindness, and hope for myself and those around me. I invite in confidence, creativity, faith, and freedom. I connect to my authentic self and I know I am enough and I am loved. I call for clarity and strength to stay true to my authentic magic and purpose. I trust my intuition to find alignment in all areas of my life. I'm here, open, and ready.

(Sit in quiet contemplation for another 3-5 minutes.)

. . . .

Your Meditation Notes

....

Conclusion:
Now What?

Now What?

. . . .

When I first decided to write this book, I was quickly overwhelmed with all kinds of self-doubt. All I could hear was the voice of my inner-critic telling me that I shouldn't do it—that nobody would care about what I had to say, that I didn't have the authority to write a book in the first place, and that if I did ultimately write this book nobody would read it anyway. But deep down, I knew in my heart that this project was calling to me—it was the next step I needed to take in my life and in my career of helping women claim their authentic power and trust their intuition in order to change the world. I HAD to do it.

So I decided to play big. Despite all my fears and discouraging thoughts, I set the intention to write and publish this book.

And Sisters, guess what happened? The universe sent me help. All the help I needed, in fact, in the form of a team of women who came together to write, read, edit, illustrate, guide, support, and fund this book. This book was created by women just like you, for women just like you—and it happened with more flow, less effort, more ease, and fewer obstacles than I could have dreamed of. All because I decided to play big, push through my fears, and trust in the universe.

Sometimes, all it takes to change your life is a little support from the Sisterhood.

That sisterhood I'm talking about—you're a part of it now. By taking this book in your hands, absorbing its messages, sharing its wisdom, and discovering all the ways it can apply to your own life, you've chosen to align yourself with a badass group of Alpha Women who are stepping out into the world with courage, trusting the abundance of the universe, manifesting the lives they desire, and maybe even changing the world a little bit along the way. Every time you take a step forward, transform your mindset, revoke power from your fears, raise your vibration, and share your authentic self with the world, we're behind you now. (You might not see us, but oh Sister, we're there. And honestly, we think you totally rock.)

So now, fellow Alpha, I ask you, with this book in your hands and the Sisterhood behind you: how are you going to take the first step towards playing it big, powering past your fears and self-doubt, and manifesting the life of your dreams?

. . . .

Special Thanks

....

Sarah Riddle Culclasure
illustrations & design
riddledesignco.com

E Ce Miller
editing & writing Support
seventhsliterary.com

Meldon Jones
editing
meldonjones.com

Sylvia Mallory
fundraising & marketing
support
sylviamalloy.com

Keri-Rae Barnum
publishing support
newshelves.com

Sarah Choi
encouragement & love
ignitecollectiveco.com
sarahchoi.rocks

Michelle Mercurio
encouragement & love
michellemercurio.com

Sophie Thomas
proofreading
sophiebthomas.com

Alpha Female Sisterhood

and

Mike Kelleher for his endless love, patience, humor, and belief
in me.

What is Alpha Female Sisterhood?

....

A community. A collective. A bunch of badass Boss Women. And so much more.

Alpha Female Sisterhood is a collective of empowering, successful Sisters who gather together in the real world and the digital one to support one another, provide guidance and healing, and share ideas and resources (or sometimes just a really great meme). Often there's Tarot. Very often, there are snacks. Every once in awhile we'll pick some once-in-a-lifetime destination across the globe and meet up there. Usually, you can find us in our home offices, inspiring each other across the airwaves.

Founded in 2016 by Seo Kelleher, the Alpha Female Sisterhood is a space where like-minded, high-performing women are invited to embrace their intuition, boost their alpha game, and expand their life, businesses and careers.

We hold each other accountable. We remind each other that we're all meant for big things.

We feature all kinds of weekly goodies in our Facebook group including: weekly intuitive coaching posts filled with tips, tricks, and strategies for expansion and greater success; psychic guidance, energy healing, and mindset tips to nourish balance, control, and abundance; Facebook Live events filled with even *more* unique support and guidance; and—oh yeah—plenty of high vibrations and butt-kicking motivation.

Basically, we want all Alpha Women to become deeply grounded in their purpose, thereby becoming even more wildly successful than they already are. We're 2,100 members strong and counting, and we want you to join us.

Doesn't that sound like something you want to be a part of? Join the sisterhood:

f **facebook.com/groups/alphafemalesisterhood**

◙ **instagram.com/alpha_female_sisterhood**

Blog: www.couragetobe.com/blog

....

About the Author

....

$$\mathcal{Seo\,Kelleher}$$

Seo Kelleher is a coach, spiritual mentor, and the founder of Alpha Female Sisterhood—a community for high-performing women to support one another, embrace their intuition, expand their careers, and share guidance and healing. In her personal and professional life she empowers women to move beyond their comfort zones, manifest abundance, and play big. As a coach, Kelleher goes beyond strategy and embraces the woo to help women change their lives so they can change the world. She believes all women can build the lives they want to live and achieve happiness and success in mind, body, and soul. *Don't Be A B*tch, Be An Alpha* is her first book.

....

- 🔲 **facebook.com/groups/alphafemalesisterhood**
- 🔲 **facebook.com/coach.seokelleher**
- 🔲 **instagram.com/alpha_female_sisterhood**
- 🔲 **instagram.com/seokelleher**

Made in United States
North Haven, CT
24 February 2023

33090063R10087